Learning to Teach with a Hangover

Also available from Continuum

How to Teach with a Hangover – Fred Sedgwick
Inside Guide to Training as a Teacher – Jon Barbuti
The Trainee Teacher's Survival Guide – Hazel Bennett

Learning to Teach with a Hangover

Jon Barbuti

continuum

Continuum International Publishing Group

The Tower Building
11 York Road
London SE1 7NX

80 Maiden Lane
Suite 704
New York, NY 10038

British Library Cataloguing-in-Publication Data
A catalogue record for this book is available from the British Library.

ISBN 0–8264–9233–9 (paperback)

Typeset by RefineCatch Limited, Bungay, Suffolk
Printed and bound in Great Britain by
Antony Rowe Ltd, Chippenham, Wiltshire

Contents

Acknowledgements

This book is dedicated to everyone who has ever got me drunk, left me broke and kept me up late at night. One person stands alone at the top of this group – my wife Ali.

Introduction

Training to be a teacher is ridiculously hard work. Even if you attend every lecture, read every book, never once enter a pub or nightclub, take a vow of celibacy for the year and go to bed at 7 p.m. religiously, it will place unimaginable demands on you.

I know this from observing some of my own course-mates, the ones whose lives seemed to consist of eating, sleeping, teacher-training and absolutely nothing else (certainly not cracking a smile). Even these A-grade, compulsively dedicated and, to use the language of the playground (as this is a book about teaching), swottish trainees struggled. Some dropped out; others became virtual mutes; still others started resembling extras from a George Romero zombie movie. And so if these seemingly perfect students struggle, what hope is there for the rest of us?

Most students like a drink, have the odd late night,

start and break new relationships, skip a few lectures, shirk the odd essay and are generally less than perfect. Some have worries that are greater still – financial concerns which necessitate the taking of a part-time job, relationship or marriage break-ups, death in the family and a whole host of other issues which contrive to make a day in class seem like a mere triviality.

On a normal course, these distractions are often little more than an irrelevance or a passing problem. Most courses merely require you to read the books, attend lectures and seminars, write essays and pass tests. Missing the odd lecture doesn't really matter in the greater scheme of things, turning up hungover or overtired to a seminar is also of little concern. All the course requires is that you pick up the notes and then revise from them at a later date when you feel better able to work.

Teacher-training courses are almost unique in that there is very little down-time. Whereas most courses, either vocational or academic, can be seen (at least by less-dedicated students), as periods of rest punctuated by occasional assessment, on teacher-training courses the pressure is relentless. During the time spent in school, the trainee has to develop an astonishing array of new skills, all the while coping with near-constant assessment as they work towards completing the much-hated standards. The time in college, which by rights should be more restful, offers little let-up, as there are essays and projects to be completed for each subject and the art of teaching to be learned. Everything taught in college is of importance.

Whereas on a history course you could focus on a few areas, shirking others knowing that you could choose from a wide range of questions in the final exam and ignore the ones you hadn't bothered to revise, teaching offers no such liberties. Topics on the course include differentiation, classroom-management, teaching English and planning engaging lessons. The trainee who skimps in one area will find themselves in trouble: after all you can hardly become a great teacher if you know all about differentiation but can't stop the classroom from descending into a scene from *Zulu*.

All this is unlikely to be news to you, though. The one thing that anyone approaching a teacher-training course knows is that it is going to be hard work. Other teachers tell you that; they bang the point home relentlessly on interview day; the early lectures have a unifying message that it's going to be incredibly difficult and the attitude of other students only serves further to emphasize the point.

On my second day on the course, I wandered into the campus library to see how many copies of certain course books were available. I didn't have any real intention of getting them out at this stage, I was just keen to get acquainted with the library, having taken three months to make the first visit to my undergraduate library and a further six to discover that it had an underground floor where 99 per cent of the books for my course were stored. What I discovered in my search for teaching books was that the library was fantastically stocked, or at least it was until about 11 a.m. the previous day. In the space of a few hours, hundreds of course-books had been taken out on long-term loans, including all 30 copies of the main prescribed text. In a fit of panic, I made a dash for the teaching section and picked up a selection of the remaining books, most of which turned out to be completely useless (especially the one written in 1957 and focusing on teaching English as a foreign language in Commonwealth countries). Four months later, the books went back, mostly unread, but with an accompanying cheque for being a month overdue. The reason that I and my fellow students were so conscientious so early was simple – there is so much to cram in that it's important to get started straightaway.

The books that I did read at this stage had broadly similar messages. They looked at how to improve your teaching; they looked at the issues involved with teaching (or the issues that were prevalent in 1937 when a couple of the books I read were published); they looked towards future trends in education. They also examined the political landscape, compared teaching in different countries and studied teaching across the Key Stages. In short, they were great at looking at the institution of teaching, terrible at looking at the teacher as an individual.

They all seemed to assume perfect knowledge and a monk-like dedication to teaching. Teaching, and this is a message banged home on the course as well as in books, is more of a lifestyle than a job. It is all-encompassing and allows for no distractions.

Except life is rarely that simple and so that is where this book comes in. Rather than take the moral high ground, assume perfect knowledge or expect trainees to have read this and 37 other course-texts, this book takes a more realistic viewpoint. The teacher-training course can be a messy experience – this book acts as the mopping-up process.

Problems will arise, be they in school, in college or as part of your (no doubt) complex personal life. The aim of this book is to help you deal with the problems, work through them and show that everyone has similar concerns. My year on the teacher-training course was full of stress and anxiety (as I will painfully recount in later chapters) and yet I'm still smiling. Just about. There's no reason why the barriers placed between you and a career in teaching should cause anything more than a slight stumble.

I won't patronize you by saying that it is all character-building – there's only so much character-building you need after all – but it is all good preparation. I am reliably informed that teaching doesn't get all that much easier even once you have qualified: the assessment and planning still place great demands on your time; the government initiatives continue to wear you down. Against this backdrop it is perhaps not all that bad that the course is hard work and, at times, almost unmanageable. If you had wanted an easy career you would not have chosen teaching, or at least you shouldn't have.

However, to be forewarned is not necessarily to be forearmed. I knew, or at least I thought I knew, that the course and the training year would be demanding before it started and yet, in hindsight, I had no real idea as to just how hard it would be. Before going into the course, I had worked in a relatively high-pressure job for five years and yet even that did not prepare me for what, to the outsider, is just another student doss. At extreme moments I considered quitting; at others I felt completely drained of all energy or that teaching was only one of myriad worries. Fortunately, I soon discovered that I was far from being alone in going through the complete gamut of emotions. Unfortunately for you, there is every chance that you too will be put through the emotional wringer.

And so the real question is not whether you will face problems, but what you should do when they arise. What's the best strategy for coping with a hangover while trying to control a class of 35 screaming kids? How can you get out of the Catch 22 situation where you're overtired but have work piled up and so find yourself working ever later into the night? What should you do if the training salary is nowhere near enough to pay the bills, but there is barely enough time to complete the course, let alone to take on a part-time job.

These are questions that you will not find answered in standard course-texts, but you will in this book. While on the training course I was dedicated to two things – gaining my teaching qualification and researching the potential problems faced by trainees. I went to the pub not to get drunk or to watch West Brom v. Spurs and play pool, but to find out what the effects would be on my teaching the next day. Similarly, I took a part-time job not because I needed the money (though it was nice), but just to see whether it was physically possible to magic another eight hours from an already overcrowded diary. Finally, I even went to great lengths to discover whether it's possible to undertake life-changing events while planning for a week in school. Admittedly I bottled out of my initial plan for a gender reassignment, but I did manage to fit a wedding into the course, even going into school just a day after my nuptials. (Now that's what I call dedication.)

All of this 'research' means that I know what can go wrong and therefore have strategies for dealing with problems. I may not be the best teacher in the world, and I don't profess to offer any great academic insight (there are millions of other books to do that in any case). What I can offer is practical 'been there, done it' advice. I have turned up to school with a raging hangover, have gone a week with barely any sleep, have tried to take on far too much and have seen others trying to deal with the fallout from crumbling relationships.

Given that you've read this far, I'm guessing that you might be someone who may also be prone to the odd lapse, or be worried that you can't survive an entire year without the odd mini-crisis. All I'd say to you is, don't panic – things are rarely as bad as they seem. In the following chapters I will aim to put a few things into perspective, to offer some friendly advice and to show you that however big a balls-up you make, it will probably pale into insignificance compared to some of the problems I managed (and still manage) to impose on myself.

To start with, I will look at what is perhaps the biggest problem of all. One where you feel like death, have an overriding sense of guilt and self-pity and take on a paranoid state in which you imagine that you will be found out and sent packing from school and the course. I am talking of hangovers, nature's way of punishing you for daring to have too much of a good time on a teacher-training course.

I can't promise to make the hangover disappear, but coping with one is an area in which I can speak with some authority. I suggest you don some dark glasses and take an Alka-Seltzer, after that we'll be ready to begin.

1 Learning to Teach with a Hangover

Is there anything more miserable than a hangover? Not only does a proper hangover – and by proper I mean the sort brought about by drinking until you think you can drink no more and then drinking another seven pints – feel like a slow, lingering death must feel, it is also the one complaint for which it is impossible to get sympathy.

Go into school with a cold and twenty people will ask if you are all right; claim you have a headache and there will be sympathetic cooing in the staffroom (in fact I even saw teachers being treated like returning soldiers when they mentioned that they had picked up a knock playing Sunday league football). However, mention a hangover and you won't get any sympathy at all. Clearly this is patently unfair. I went into school hungover a number of times, whether under the guise of research for this book, or as the result of a post-college study session where we got sidetracked and started drinking, or just because I fancied a night off planning and so went to the pub instead. On each and every occasion I had to pretend that either there was nothing wrong, or to pass it off as a migraine. On one occasion I even had to sink the migraine medicine handed me by a concerned teaching-assistant – a move which, given my subsequent six-hour stint spent doubled over the toilet-bowl, was perhaps a tad unwise.

And so you suffer in silence. I would suggest that however bad your hangover, even if every noise makes you want to cut off your ears, do not tell anyone in school why you are ailing. Among the staff, it will be impossible to get any sympathy for a problem which is self-inflicted. Personally, I've never fully understood this point of view. Admittedly the problem was avoidable, but hangovers are far from being the only illness – and given how bad they feel I think it's fair to call hangovers an illness – which occur due to human weakness. Skiing injuries are caused by adrenaline junkies overstretching themselves on the piste; a variety of strains are the direct result of people failing to keep themselves in shape; many headaches occur simply because the eyes have been forced to watch hours of television. It would hardly be acceptable to say of a cancer victim 'Oh, but they deserve it because they smoked all their lives', and yet hangovers are portrayed in school as being the price that has to be paid for daring to drink.

Learning to Teach with a Hangover

In most jobs (lumberjacks and counsellors at Alcoholics Anonymous excepted) you can get away with being hungover simply by getting your head down and keeping out of your colleagues' way for the day. And the same can be true in teaching, only not for the trainee. For the experienced teacher, going into school still hungover presents problems – the head to be avoided, the parents to be dealt with as painlessly as possible, the letters to be remembered – but these are nothing compared to the perils awaiting the hungover trainee.

The problem for the trainee teacher is that they feel (and often are) on trial. Once you have qualified and are safely ensconced in your own classroom, coming in hungover occasionally may pose less of a problem. You will control the class and set tasks with your headache in mind – extended writing, reams of sums, watching a video. Anything that means that they can just be left to their own devices as much as possible. These tasks may not win you any teacher of the year awards, but they will at least help you through a painful few hours, and that is the aim of this chapter. Obviously we'd all love to be a great teacher, but there are times when it's best to admit that you'd struggle to teach GCSE physics to Stephen Hawkins. At these times your focus should be on survival, both in terms of getting through the day and also protecting your reputation as being hardworking and reliable, or at least ensuring that your reputation doesn't take too much of a dive in the opposite direction.

Learning to Teach with a Hangover

As a qualified teacher, you have that luxury. It is your class and so if you do go in stinking of lager, with bags under your eyes and your tongue glued to the top of your mouth there's still a fair chance you can come through the day unscathed just so long as you can nip out unnoticed at 3.15 p.m. As a trainee, however, your plight will be obvious from the moment you first enter the classroom in the morning (probably late) to be greeted by the class-teacher. For the class-teacher is all-seeing. They notice when little Jimmy is fidgeting in his chair, they notice when Jane has scribbled on her text-book and they sure as hell notice when you come in resembling something out of *The Evil Dead*.

To be honest, they have probably been waiting for the moment when you roll in worse for wear. In one of my placement schools I got the feeling that I was never entirely welcome in class, that I was someone who had been imposed on the teacher. Some teachers are great and are genuinely keen to pass on their knowledge and to see the trainee grow (and perhaps to see their own workload reduced significantly for a few weeks), but others see the trainee as a burden. They probably had the trainee imposed on them, the school signing up because it gets extra funding for taking on trainees and the staff would much rather teach their own lessons than have to suffer a spotty youth coming in and teaching lessons which they'll see as a pale imitation of their own. They will have targets to hit, be it in the form of SATs or other end-of-year assessments and will probably see it as hard enough to hit those even with a full year teaching the class. Being taken out of the firing-line, to be replaced by a novice for key periods only serves to increase the chances that the class will fall slightly behind schedule. To them, to use a sporting analogy, it must feel like being Wayne Rooney only to be taken off at half-time and replaced by Peter Crouch – a change that, in their eyes, has no perceptible benefit whatsoever.

But I don't mean to be harsh on the class-teacher. Their feelings, assuming of course that they do feel this negativity (and many teachers don't; they are truly wonderful towards the trainee), are entirely natural. If you're falling at all short in your lessons there will be an inevitable knock-on effect when it comes to assessment. However, when the time comes for someone to be held accountable it will be the teacher left answering the awkward questions. The trainee will have left long before to enjoy an extended summer of drinking and job-searching. And so the hungover trainee both comes as justification and an excuse.

The fact that you have turned up hungover will instantly validate any resentment that they may have towards leaving you in charge of the class. Not only is the class now being taught by someone without experi-ence, it is being taught, in their eyes, by someone who is unprofessional. And of course the fact that you have turned up hungover gives them a perfect excuse for any failings that the class might have, how could they be expected to hit SATs targets when the trainee that came in fell below the expected standards. Only, they won't just think this, they'll communicate it to everyone that matters – the teaching-assistants, the other teachers, your mentor and probably the head.

The gossip prevalent in schools, especially with relation to trainees, is perhaps all the motivation needed to avoid ever turning up hungover. One boozy evening can have serious implications on your entire placement – not because it could lead to you failing (the odd slip isn't that serious), but because it can create a negative atmosphere for your spell in school. With the ultimate aim of the training course being to find employment, a reputation for turning up hungover, even if based on just one incident, can wreak havoc. Your placement school, the place where you should have the inside track on any vacancy, is unlikely to employ you if your class-teacher has told the head, and possibly the governors and anyone else who will listen, that you have turned up half-cocked.

But the pain doesn't necessarily end there. Even if getting a job at your placement school is not an option – there might not be one available, there might be one that you're not suitable for or you might just not fancy teaching at a school where you've been made to feel like a rat in a restaurant – you might still need their help. In appointing a trainee, most schools will be keen to get references from your placement schools and a write up that reads 'has a tendency to wander in pissed' doesn't tend to go down too well. And that's if it even gets that far. School heads tend to be like brothers and sisters in Alabama, having more knowledge of each other than you might otherwise imagine. In this incestuous setting, rumour and gossip spreads like wildfire, and rather than go through that whole reference rigmarole, schools will often simply ring your placement school prior to interview to get the low-down on your abilities, with regard to teaching, time-keeping and drinking that is.

One final problem to consider is the impact a few boozy sessions can have on your reputation on the course. I don't mean among your peers – having spent many hours holed up in the pub with me, mine were probably under no illusions that I suffered from a deadly combination of loving beer and not really being able to handle it very well. No, I mean among the lecturers and tutors. You might not need their friendship and you might not even need the advice given out by some of them, but you probably will need references at some stage. If your placement school and personal tutor are both unwilling to write a reference without including the words 'tendency, late, stinking and drunk' then finding a job will become as difficult as following snooker on a black-and-white television – a bad analogy admittedly, but one that seems fairly relevant as it's exactly what I'm doing at this moment.

But, as I watch an unknown Welshman missing a simple

red (or was it the black), I realize that this chapter has become far too negative. It's full of what might go wrong if you turn up hungover, and yet you are probably all too aware of the potential pitfalls. One of the key differences between hangovers and other ailments is the fact that there is always the fear of being found out. With most ailments, it is marvellous when people notice just how ill you are. You get brownie-points for actually turning up (as long as you haven't infected half the school with the flu) and you might even get sent home early. As someone who turned up ill only to be sent home, I can assure you that getting an unexpected afternoon off is pure bliss. Especially when you get back in time for *Ready, Steady, Cook* and even more especially when the lesson you had planned for the afternoon was, to use a technical term, bobbins. And even if you don't get sent home, being ill acts as a licence to perform a little below your best, which, as a trainee, can be manna from heaven as the odd lesson is bound to bomb regardless of your health.

With hangovers there is a horrible feeling that you're going to be caught at any moment. For me, it reminds me of being back in primary school, specifically to a time when I had written the word 'twit' in giant chalk letters on the playground floor (it was a very polite school). At the time, it seemed like an ingenious way of catching people in our school's version of 'tag', but for the rest of the day, and indeed week, I then had to worry about being found out. And of course I was discovered and got a lecture from the head. Apparently, writing rude words on the playground is not the sort of behaviour expected of trainee teachers.

This is the feeling which prevails as a trainee. Feeling ill is bad enough, but what is much worse is having to hide the symptoms because the pain of discovery would be far worse than the pain of the hangover (hard though that may be to imagine at the time). During my training year, I went in hungover a number of times and only on one occasion did I dare disclose my discomfort.

The time in question was an anomaly and, bizarrely, I seemed to get brownie-points simply for turning up. All sympathy was well deserved, though, as it was, without question, the worst hangover in history. To set the scene, all week I had been looking forward to Friday, which, to be fair, was pretty typical of most weeks. However, on this occasion, the feeling was almost overwhelming. It was early on in the course, my first full week in school and yet my mind was elsewhere. Every second was spent dreaming of the beer and debauchery that would come at the weekend as I said farewell to the single life in the time-honoured manner of getting as disgracefully, irresponsibly and outrageously drunk as is humanly possible. Knowing that if I turned up at all on Monday (I had visions of finding myself naked on a Normandy beach) I would be in no real state to do anything other than make a neat pile of drawl by my feet, I had informed both my class-teacher and tutor of my plans for the weekend.

And I would recommend this course of action if you have an event planned from which it is impossible to return sober. The school may not like being told that you will be in no fit state to teach on the Monday, but it is probably better to prepare them for the worst, rather than to give them a nasty surprise. Schools are run in a strictly ordered fashion, and surprises seem to be the single thing that many heads like the least. A bird flying into the hall during one of my placements had the effect of turning the entire school into an amateur dramatics version of *Birds*: the entire school was evacuated into the playground with grown adults flapping around as if the aliens had landed. This problem was then exacerbated as the sun came out and, although it was only March and still decidedly chilly, the whole cohort had to be moved again, to the side of a building and a two-metre square patch of land to be kept away from our nearest star's harmful rays.

It was against this sort of backdrop that I calmly told the school that I would be turning up bladdered and, all things considered, they took it pretty well. The class-teacher even offered (an offer I was to snap up in less than a second) to teach my lessons on the Monday while I just sat and observed. And so, when the time came, observing is exactly what I did, though not the class. My gaze was centred on my shoes and the reflection of the light bulb bouncing across their newly polished surface. At the time it seemed fascinating, a bit like the time when, as an awkward 10-year-old, I pretended to be mute as a ruse to avoid being brought into a conversation.

The class-teacher said nothing about my near-comatose state. (I think I had the look of someone who it was severely unwise to mess with.) To put my mood into context, on the Friday of my stag do, I arrived in Nottingham at 6 p.m. and proceeded straight to the hotel bar, even this presenting a mission as I had already had five cans on the train over. A couple of hours in the hotel bar were followed by several more hours stuck in the corner of a pub chosen entirely because of its proximity to the hotel and McDonald's. Several hours later, after more beer than I'd drunk in the previous twelve months, we moved onto some identikit club or other and then the real drinking started. After that, my memory of the night is somewhat hazy, though anyone wanting photos of the night is more than welcome to email me on jon.barbuti@ntlworld.com. For those who don't email, the photos show me dancing (very badly), drinking (but spilling most of it) and watching as my wife-to-be's brother, supposedly there to keep an eye on me, chatted up a series of middle-aged Nottingham women.

And that was just the warm-up night.

Day Two was, to be honest, just a blur. First up was

hungover paint-balling, which is like normal paint-balling only with the added hilarity of shooting your own teammates in the back from inches away. Rather impressively if you ask me, I still bear the scars from the experience. During one challenge I was shot in the head by one so-called friend from no more than a yard away, then, when I put my hand up to acknowledge being out the game, was shot in the hand from a range of five centimetres. My hand instantly swelled up and, for a number of weeks, resembled a mini-target, as if some particularly talented hamsters had been practising their archery skills by aiming at it.

The rest of the day, to avoid going into needless detail, consisted of drinking and yet more drinking, be it drinking at the pub watching the football, drinking at the pool hall, drinking with our meal, drinking at the dogs or drinking in the club. Especially drinking in the club, where one kindly soul bought me two double Aftershocks which I had to mix and down. Given that my heart-rate immediately tripled, I started speaking in tongues and then ran around the club imitating a bee, I would advise anyone else thinking of drinking copious amounts of what is probably the most potent pick-me-up in the world to think again.

In total, I drank more than my own weight in alcohol that weekend and so even by Monday, having had Sunday to recover, I was still barely able to muster the energy to breathe. In fact, that whole week was a bit of a write-off (as indeed were several others in that school, but that's a whole different issue).

Not all hangovers are of the 'hmm, would it be easier to open my eyes the normal way or by using my fingers' variety. While on the course, I experienced a fair few, what I would term 'common or garden hangovers'. For these I blame my course-mates. I would suggest we meet up somewhere to discuss the course or our time in school and, somehow, somewhere always turned into the pub. Equally surprisingly, the conversation always drifted away from the initial topic and into more random areas – rating the pub's choice of crisps, trying to remember the names of the more anonymous course-mates, picking an England XI made up entirely of players whose surname was related to meat (Barry Venison being the honorary captain). Each of these sessions only consisted of a handful of pints, but when you are tired and have to work when you get home this is more than enough to bring on a fierce hangover the following morning. And it is these hangovers which you really have to worry about far more than the humdingers brought about by a major bender. After all, when your bar bill for the weekend is bigger than your mortgage you expect to feel the after-effects, but when all you have done is go out and sink five pints the resultant headache feels both unfair and unjustified. There is also a degree of randomness to these hangovers. Some days you can go out, get drunk and wake up the next morning feeling fine; whereas other nights you drink far less and yet have a hangover out of all proportion.

And yet this seeming randomness is not actually random at all. The extent of your hangover is, to a large extent, determined by factors completely unrelated to how much you have drunk. If you are generally tired and run-down, you are far more susceptible to illness, and the same is true of hangovers. One of the main pieces of advice I would offer to avoid hangovers is simply not to drink when you are overtired. Of course you could just not drink at all, but if you were that sort of person you probably wouldn't have picked up this book, or if you did it would just be to scoff and mutter 'Disgraceful. Encouraging teachers to drink . . .'. No, assuming that, like me, the prospect of not drinking for a year is enough to make you instantly start drinking, you can at least try to limit your intake. If you are feeling tired or remotely unwell, simply do not go near alcohol as it is the exact opposite of what your body needs. Rest up, get an early night and eat some fruit and veg and you may well feel significantly better by the morning. Drink, and things will only get much worse – and don't even think that taking the day off sick will make it all right. That phone call you have to make at 8 a.m., when you put on the fake croaky voice and say how you've been up all night with a migraine is every bit as stressful as a day in school. Everyone knows when someone is faking an illness and your feeble attempts at pretending to be on death row will fool no one. And, incidentally, why do people always speak in a pathetic voice when they are feigning an illness? When taking the occasional what Americans call 'duvet-day', I've used a voice that sounds like Jane Horrocks with laryngitis, and yet genuine illnesses have never once caused my voice to turn all pathetic. Perhaps it's just because none of us quite has the balls to ring in with a confident 'I feel ill and won't be in today. Goodbye.'

As well as the longer-term effects of illness and tiredness, there are myriad short-term factors which will also determine whether or not you get a hangover and, if you do, just how debilitating it will be.

I'd always secretly scoffed at my brother's habit of getting a pint of water to go with his pint, and I particularly hated having to go to the bar to ask for a pint of water. In terms of things you don't ask a barman for, water is second only to orange squash. Frankly, if you only have 50 pence to spend you shouldn't go to a bar – you should save up until you can afford a proper drink. He claimed that having six pints of water would ensure that you stayed hydrated and thus see off any hangover the following morning. (This being before the time I started having to work for a living, his advice was an irrelevance. Any hangover could be slept off the next morning and then topped up again with a spell in the student bar.)

Even when I started working as a journalist I never really bothered drinking water to stave off a hangover.

Learning to Teach with a Hangover

Unlike teaching, journalism still has a certain machismo attached to it, and walking in a few minutes late with puffy eyes and five o'clock shadow does not pose any significant problems. In any case, there's always a fair chance that the boss will wander in a few minutes later looking even worse, and so everyone just gets their heads down, feels sorry for themselves and drinks copious amounts of viscous coffee.

Teaching is from the opposite end of the spectrum. Whereas as a reporter you can take a certain pride in your hangover as it shows that you're conforming to the hackneyed cliché of the drunk newshound, the clichés concerning teaching all centre on respectable motherly types working in an environment where drinking is severely frowned upon. Having learned quickly that the classroom was no place to take a hangover and realizing that simply not drinking was out of the question, it was time to try my brother's advice.

And guess what. The know-it-all was right. He was right whenever he predicted he would beat me at tennis (I don't think I've beaten him more than once in 100 matches); he was right whenever he said he'd beat me at pool (though the worm has turned on that score); and he was right when he claimed that drinking huge quantities of water staved off hangovers. There is still one problem with this method, though – remembering to drink the water. If you're anything like me, as I have said, you simply don't like drinking water in a pub. If you get there at 7 p.m. you have maybe four hours to drink, but once you've factored in conversation, trips to the loo and the odd game on the fruit machine; this is cut in half. With just two hours left, why would you want to divide this in half by drinking water as well as beer? Simply put, being a lightweight it takes me a fair while to drink a pint, so the last thing I want to be doing is wasting time drinking water. This leaves two options: drink water before going out or when you get back.

However, only one of these options ever actually works in my experience. You can go out with the best intentions of drinking water when you get home, but at some stage the plan goes out the window. Instead of sitting on the couch downing mineral water, you find yourself watching some terrible old horror movie (usually *The Fog*), eating a kebab and drinking another can. Even when I have managed to drink water when I get in, it has been in such inconsequential quantities (usually one small glass) that it makes absolutely no difference to the following morning's hangover.

Drinking water before going out is far more practical and it can even have the added bonus of filling your stomach, thus limiting the amount of alcohol you can drink (or at least the amount you can down without having to run off to the toilet every two minutes). However, you have to drink a lot. One pint of water is not going to make any difference, ideally you'll need to drink a pint of water for every pint (or drink of similar alcoholic content) that you enjoy. Think of it either as a necessary evil in order to enjoy your evening or as a challenge. I liked to think of myself as Paul Newman in *Cool Hand Luke*, only with pints of water replacing hardboiled eggs, but that's just me. And I'm sad.

A word of caution about drinking water to avoid hangovers. You have to do it on the day of the drinking. If you wake up hungover, there is no amount of water which will make you feel better or flush the feelings out of the system. I know this through experimentation for this book (how I suffer for my work). All you'll succeed in doing is making yourself feel even more sick with a bloated stomach to complement your banging head. Also, don't take aspirin, ibuprofen or any similar painkiller to stave off hangovers, as these can apparently have some pretty dire consequences in extreme cases, including liver failure and (possibly), death. Your body is already struggling to cope with all the alcohol that needs to be broken down: mixing a fairly powerful drug into this cocktail is a pretty stupid idea when you stop to think about it.

Sadly, avoiding a hangover isn't quite as simple as just drinking water, though that will make a significant difference. As well as ensuring that you are hydrated, it is also important that you are nourished. Going out drinking on an empty stomach ensures two things. Firstly that you will wake up with a head that feels as if Dennis Quaid has recreated *Inner Space* by parking his mini spaceship in your brain and is carrying out some major construction work. It will also lead to you going to some dodgy takeaway, probably called something like 'Licking Chickins', 'Donner you Feel Hungry' or 'A Pizza the Action' and buying the greasiest, most calorific item on a menu that seems to have been drawn up with the sole intention of upping the local heart-attack rate. I'm not sure which of these is the worst, but for the moment we'll concentrate on the hangover.

With an empty stomach, there is nothing to help soak the alcohol up and so it hardly takes a doctor to tell you that the booze will have more of an impact, which is fortunate as I'm not a doctor. The advice is equally obvious. Make sure you eat before embarking on a drinking session, or at least while you're drinking. If drinking time is limited, which it still tends to be in Britain, why not go all continental and enjoy a meal with a drink. You could even pretend you're French by having a glass of red wine (the watering-down is optional) with your burger-in-a-bun. As with drinking water, if you fail to eat at the time there is little point thinking that having a big meal in the morning will improve your situation. Some people swear that a greasy fry-up acts as a cure for hangovers and it's a method you're welcome to try, but the one time I ate sausage, bacon and egg with a hangover I ended up with more on the plate than I started with.

In fact, there is a wealth of supposed hangover cures which seem to work for some people and not for others.

Learning to Teach with a Hangover

One that I have perfected is to exercise myself back to full health. It's a method that I stumbled across by accident at Swansea University. Forgetting that I had an early morning football match the following morning, I drank myself to oblivion one Saturday night. (I was so drunk that I walked into a door, chipping a bone in my finger, yet didn't notice the injury until the next morning.) Anyway, Sunday morning came and I was barely able to move, let alone stand, on the right wing waiting for the ball to come to me. Eventually, though, the ball came to me and I had to set off on a sprint to try to beat my marker. Sprinting turned out to be a very bad idea as I was hit by a feeling that felt like being punched in the stomach and so I pulled up and promptly threw up on the side of the pitch. Incredibly, having thrown up, I instantly felt better and had one of my best-ever games. (I must have touched the ball at least seven times in 90 minutes.) Since then, I have always tried to go for a run or to the gym if I feel hungover, though it's obviously wise to avoid being sick on the plush gym floor (especially when the staff all resemble 18-stone gorillas).

And while the exercise method works for me, there are numerous other hangover cures which people swear by. Tomatoes, the must-haves of cheap salads the world over, can have miraculous recuperative powers: According to some reports, they can quell even the worst of hangovers within an hour.

A remedy which has more basis in scientific fact

(though as someone who runs himself to sickness, I'm not sure I can take the scientific high ground) is to take vitamin B12. In drinking, and I'm taking this as fact as my dietary knowledge is awful, you deplete your B12 levels and this is, at least partly, what causes you to feel terrible the following morning. Simply taking a B12 supplement or two, either when you get in or the following morning, can go a long way towards lifting the hangover (though it can't negate the problems brought about by dehydration). Similarly, just eating a healthy diet, or at least taking regular multi-vitamin supplements, leaves your body in much better shape to fight off the effects of a hangover. If it's already fighting a cold and the debilitating effects of a poor diet, then it simply won't have any resources left to fight the hangover – the one thing that you really want it to be fighting.

Most other remedies I have come across also come from a fairly sound basis of trying to replenish your body with all the stuff that the alcohol has taken out. Red Bull, which may have been mixed with its natural bedfellow Mr Vodka to create all the problems in the first place, is actually quite good at kicking you back into action. A glance at the side of a Red Bull can shows that it's full of an endless mix of ingredients and additives, and so it's perhaps no surprise that at least a few of these are beneficial. In much the same way as if you have enough monkeys typing away you'll come away with a decent book eventually, if you throw enough ingredients into a drink

Learning to Teach with a Hangover

at least a few will combine in an unexpected way to produce something of value. It's a technique I mastered as a six-year-old wannabe chef, throwing every ingredient I could find (including Worcester sauce and mustard) into a chocolate sauce. (It tasted considerably better than Red Bull, though.)

Along similar lines is the method of taking anything with a high sugar content the following morning. Honey, which personally I can't stand, and ice pops, which fortunately I love, both replenish your fructose levels and leave you feeling much better. An added benefit of this is that it gives you the perfect excuse to suck on six freeze pops on your way to school, though you might get the occasional odd look if, like me, you find yourself eating them at 7 a.m. on a train in the middle of January.

If the thought of eating anything while hungover is abhorrent, then you at least need to settle your stomach. The exercise method, I mentioned earlier works pretty well for this, but given that eating is out the question I doubt you'll feel like hitting the gym. Milk can, supposedly, help settle the stomach, though it's not a method which has worked for me. Similarly, drinking milk before embarking on the boozing has only limited success and probably only works in part because it at least stops the body from becoming too dehydrated and slows down the rate at which alcohol is absorbed.

A far more effective stomach settler is Alka-Seltzer. If you can get past the vile taste, you'll find Alka-Seltzer to be a little miracle-worker as it gets to work almost immediately and starts ironing out the aches and pains which accompany a hangover. You could also try ginger beer, but make sure you buy a brand which lists ginger root among the ingredients.

The key point to take from this chapter is to learn how to manage a hangover. The complete prevention of all hangovers is an unlikely goal: stress-levels on the course and the need to take the occasional break from planning and assessment mean that pubs and nightclubs become irresistibly appealing. However, if you're going to drink you need to do so confident in the knowledge that you'll at least be able to do a passable job the following morning.

To do so, there are just two basic steps. Firstly, make sure that your body is prepared for the alcohol onslaught by drinking water and eating a healthy meal. If you're in any way under the weather, call the night off.

Secondly, plan your recovery. Ensure that you are well stocked with fruit, Red Bull, honey, ice pops, or whatever else you have chosen to replenish your body with. It doesn't really matter which method you choose (I suspect that it is largely psychosomatic in any case, and once you have found a method that works it will continue to work simply because you expect to feel better). Settling on a remedy is another matter entirely. If you're a budding science teacher you could always try one method at a time, thus treating your hangover as an

Learning to Teach with a Hangover

experiment to check out the effectivenesses of a range of hangover cures. For anyone who is more concerned with their head than the need to set up a fair experiment, I'd recommend taking pretty much anything you can. In much the same way that Red Bull works simply because it includes every substance known to man, if you cram your stomach full of potential hangover cures at least one of them is bound to do some good. And don't worry if your stomach objects and sends the remedies straight back from whence they came – you've just stumbled across my patented 'vomiting it up' method, the twin sister of my equally successful 'sick-and-run' technique.

Learning to Teach with a Hangover

If you also had little need of the first chapter, I must also apologize. You have been shortchanged by about 6,000 words and someone should pay. I'd seek redress from the publishers – their details should be at the front of the book.

But whether or not you require a chapter which, not to put too fine a point on it, tells you how to get away with turning up pissed, you will certainly need a chapter that looks at how to cope with tiredness. In a few ways, hangovers and tiredness feel all too similar. When you wake up with either ailment you are overtired, irritable, lacking in concentration and probably suffering from a headache. That, though, is where the similarities end. Compared to extreme tiredness, hangovers are a walk in the park. At worst, a hangover will affect you on one day only, and generally they are already starting to clear by lunchtime. With a hangover, you probably only have to get through three tough hours in school, which, when you factor in the mid-morning break, could be as little as two lessons. Although this may feel like a mini-lifetime it really isn't all that long in the greater scheme of things. I think the only comparable experience I've had is, unfortunately, one I'm getting all too often at present in training for a half marathon. Two hours may not sound like a long time to run, but when you are already at the stage of challenging yourself to run for another ten seconds once you've done a mile, a thirteen-mile run might as well be a trek across the Sahara without water. However, somehow I will get through the race (not that I'll be racing in the strictest, or indeed any, sense of the word). That is, of course, if my Achilles tendon doesn't snap, as it has been threatening to for some time. But I digress.

Hangovers are, by nature, short-term, and they also hint at better times. At least in getting it you had a few drinks, had a dance and quite possibly did something you might now regret with Jane from the undergraduate nursing course.

Tiredness, though it sounds fairly lightweight as problems go – it hardly ranks alongside motor-neurone disease or typhoid – is actually a far bigger problem than the humble hangover. It impinges on everything you do and can lead to a drastic drop in your own performance in the classroom. In terms of factors which really could damage your ability to complete the course successfully and find employment, I can think of nothing more serious than perennial overtiredness.

And that is what we are talking about here. Obviously every student has the odd day when they are a bit tired – a late night, a car alarm going off outside, stress because of an impending exam. However, real problems start when days turn into weeks and weeks turn into months. It is no exaggeration to say that at one stage on my training course I felt continually tired for a period of over six weeks. Only now, with the benefit of hindsight and a little research, have I any idea as to how I should have dealt with the problem. I needed to identify the symptoms early on and take corrective action there and then. By the time it got to a period of weeks, the tiredness had taken such a thorough hold that I doubt that even three straight days in bed would have left me feeling refreshed. Normal measures simply won't work once you have got to the stage of extreme exhaustion.

The best remedy is to simply stop the onset of tiredness. Of course, things aren't always quite that easy, which is both bad news for you and good news for me who have a chapter to flesh out. Teacher-training courses simply aren't designed to be a cakewalk. During five years as a sports reporter I never suffered from tiredness in the same way as I did while studying to be a teacher and this is despite having suffered some pretty horrendous hours in my job. Admittedly, most of the time my hours were strictly 9.07 a.m. to 4.58 p.m., but there was a time in 2002 when covering the Commonwealth Games meant a 7.30 a.m. start and a 1 a.m. finish for two solid weeks. Factor in travelling time, and I should have been suffering from extreme fatigue, yet I felt no more dopey than usual (which, admittedly, is quite dopey). This is because even in those long hours there were still periods of relaxation and also the stress of any individual hour was never all that great. Most of the time it was simply a case of some fairly easy coverage, or helping out in the office wherever needed – doing a job I could do in my sleep. On the teacher-training course, and especially during the time spent in school, there is never a moment to relax and so every minute takes its toll on your body.

Teaching the lessons takes a huge amount out of you during the early weeks. Physically, you have to be moving about, checking who is working, generating enthusiasm and excitement and also imposing yourself on anyone daring to misbehave. For someone used to an office job, this is a challenge in itself, as gone are the days when teachers could just sit behind their wooden desks for nine hours. Nowadays they are on their feet more than the cheering throngs at the Last Night of the Proms. On top of the physical exertion, there is also extreme mental strain, as you worry unduly about each and every minute of every lesson. During the lesson, there are worries about the timing, whether the lesson is suitable, whether it is enjoyable and whether the class are learning. After the lesson, if you're not teaching again straightaway, there is the worry of the post-mortem: your brain replaying every little mistake and turning it into far more of a problem than ever it was. These concerns then carry through into your next lesson, so that not only are you worried about delivering that lesson to the best of your ability but you are also preoccupied with concerns that you will repeat the same mistakes and so, almost inevitably, do. This pattern, repeated two or three times per day, is enough to lead to extreme mental exhaustion, and that is before the effects of planning, assessment and coursework have been factored in.

Learning to Teach with a Hangover

In most jobs, following a stressful day, there is at least a relaxing evening and the promise of a better day to be embraced. However, the trainee teacher leaves school for the evening to be faced by an evening of work in the form of planning, assessing their teaching and the classes' learning and also any outstanding coursework. Having finished that late at night (often well past midnight in my experience) they then go to bed only to get up early the next morning for the same pattern to be repeated. Is this stress worth it? In the long run, absolutely if you want to be an effective teacher; however, in the short term it can prove almost unbearable.

And the above is by no means an exaggeration. It is honestly the pattern I found myself in for a couple of weeks in my first placement and, more damagingly, two months in my second, and it is a cycle that my peers admitted to being stuck in as well. Looking back now, some of the incidents brought about by tiredness seem almost laughable, such as catching 40 winks in the staffroom at lunch-time, but at the time they were no laughing matter. In an unfriendly staffroom, you are unlikely to fall asleep unless you really cannot avoid it (especially if you have left an unopened KitKat on the table in a room full of six gannet-like teachers). Falling asleep is also unlikely to endear you to anyone in the school; in their eyes it is likely to be taken as another sign that you are struggling with the workload (a view which though quite possibly accurate is not one you'll want to promote).

Learning to Teach while Overtired

Fortunately for me, the most extreme example of tired-ness affecting my performance went entirely unnoticed by the school. It came at the height of stress season. I was by now teaching the whole timetable (leaving the class-teacher free to spend hours planning the school drama production), getting prepared for the final visit by the assessor – preparation in this instance meaning writing up hundreds of lesson-plans which at that stage only existed as scribbled notes – and also working on some essay or other. (I think it was something to do with the best ways to assess PE: an essay which had to expand greatly on my own views that PE is pretty well unassessable. How, after all, do you compare five children jumping off boxes, or measure their ability to free-form dance taking fire as their inspiration?) This in itself was a workload to guarantee extreme tiredness, but there were still a couple of little clinchers to be fitted in. Still searching for a job, I found myself trawling through the *TES* and websites every night, as well as filling out the same application forms dozens of time. (Teaching applications are as arduous as they come with each one requiring five pages of boxes to be hand-filled, the schools having worked out that if they get 20 applicants they then get 100 sheets of paper that can be used for the copying of non-essential documents, thus shaving £1.27 off their sta-tionery bill for the year.) Finally, there was also a part-time job to be fitted in. The course tutors suggest that it's impossible to fit in a part-time job while training to be a teacher, and they probably have a point, but then it can be equally impossible to live on the training salary for a year, especially if your wife is unwilling to foreclose on the house and move into cardboard city. (A chapter later in this book looks in more detail at the issue of part-time jobs on the course, but for now suffice it to say that they are just another commitment eating into the few waking hours you have available.)

With work upon work piling up, my school then decided to do the one thing which is almost guaranteed to induce sleep. They organized a day-trip to the opera. It was meant to be an opera taster especially designed for primary school children, though I suspect that tailoring opera for children is as doomed to failure as running a gin-tasting course for the under-nines. During the course of two hours, three fat men and a fat woman warbled their way through a few of the classics, only raising any interest from the kids when they seemingly forgot their audience for a minute and started simulating some adult activities. For me, however, the time simply flew by. Initially this was out of worry – an elderly, dishevelled gentleman had chosen to sit down right among the kids raising all sorts of fears (as it turned out he was part of the show). Later on it was because my mind was elsewhere, visualizing me scoring the winning goal for Gillingham in the 2006 FA Cup Final – a recurrent dream that is unlikely on an unfeasibly large number of levels. My dreaming meant that, as far as I was concerned, the show only lasted for about five minutes – it started, I worried about the man, I saw the opera singers forget themselves and then I ran onto a pass from Andy Hessenthaler and rammed home from 25 yards before waking up again. In total, I had slept on and off for around 90 minutes (which, coincidentally, is how long I sleep for at the typical Gillingham match), but I was at least lucky in that no teacher noticed – they too were dozing – and that it wasn't a teacher that woke me up. It was the pupils next to me who had started sniggering at the sound of Mr Carbooty's snoring. I was probably lucky. I am not sure what action the school would have taken; it would depend on who had noticed. Some teachers would have laughed it off; others would have seen it as a serious breach in standards; still others would have admitted that they too dozed off. Either way, falling asleep on the job can hardly be seen as a career move to be encouraged, but then that's what happens when course organizers try to place unreasonable demands on the student cohort.

The point I am making is that while falling asleep at school may not be inevitable, what is inevitable is that you will come close to it. Lessons seem to last for hours, the school day is spent just thinking about getting home and going to bed (except you can't go to bed because there's a pile of paperwork to be done) and because you lack the energy to deliver top-class lessons little things that you thought you had nailed start slipping. Class discipline can take a dive as your lethargic performance encourages the kids to play up, while lessons also lose much of their vigour as tiredness seems to promote safe, paper-based lessons rather than interesting, intensive sessions full of experimental learning which involve more planning.

This is normal tiredness or, at least, normal tiredness for the latter stages of a teacher-training course. However, that is not to say that you should simply accept it and do nothing to counter the effects. As with most illnesses, prevention is better than a cure, and again, in common with other complaints, there are a host of practical steps which can be followed to reduce the impact of tiredness.

Maintaining a balanced diet is crucial. I enjoy a takeaway pizza or curry as much as the next man (I had to wait to write that line until Johnny Vegas had moved from my side), but it is important to remember that your body is, if not a temple, at least a reasonably efficient Fiat Punto. Feed it full of junk and it will splutter, stall and eventually break down. The diet has to be balanced both in terms of nutrients, especially taking care to ensure you are getting your vitamins and minerals, and also quantity. The stress and time demands of teaching lead to many people skipping their lunch and eating a light evening meal; however, if you are not feeding your body with sufficient calories, and especially carbohydrates, it simply will not have the fuel to lift itself out of slumber.

Learning to Teach while Overtired

One of the easiest ways to ensure you are at least getting close to meeting your body's dietary demands is to invest in multivitamin and iron tablets. Popping one of these a day means that no matter how bad your diet is you will at least get close to keeping your body nourished. The importance of healthy eating really cannot be overemphasized. Having completed a hard day in school, often the last thing we feel like doing is cooking a healthy meal from scratch. It is so much easier to pull something out of the freezer for another prick-and-ping meal. And though these meals will fill you up, it won't be with anything particularly healthy, as a quick glance at the ingredients will confirm. Our bodies need vegetables, fruit, fish, meat and other naturally occurring products; they have no natural desire for E1110 or its sister E1237. (As an aside, the course tutor on a recent health and safety course I attended noted how problems such as asthma and diabetes are now far more prevalent than they were even ten years ago. He put this change entirely down to our bodies being forced to cope with a constant barrage of toxins. So, rather than reaching for the ready meal, cook something fresh. It doesn't have to be *Masterchef* style: pasta and sauce will suffice, and your body will start to thank you for it.)

Allied to healthy eating, try to live at least reasonably healthily by fitting in some exercise. In a cramped timetable, finding the time to go for a run, swim a few lengths, or to nip down the gym is hard, but make the effort and it will more than repay itself. An hour spent in semi-strenuous exercise kicks the body and mind into action to such an extent that on returning home and starting to work you will probably get more done in an hour than you would normally achieve in a whole evening. I tended to find that on the evenings that I felt there wasn't time to go to the gym (normally evenings when it was chucking it down outside) I'd pontificate and time-waste for at least an hour and end up wishing I had actually exercised if only to force my overtired body out of its well-deserved slumber. Of course, if the exercise is too strenuous it will have the opposite effect. You need to do something that is well within your capabilities and preferably focused on cardiovascular activity. Trying to set a new world record for weight-lifting will take so much out of you that you will barely be able to move on returning home, let alone knuckle down to work. (That is if you can walk home and aren't carted off to the local A&E for some treatment on a snapped muscle or two.) How often should you exercise? How long is a piece of string? Exercising every day will do more harm than good, as the body cannot recover in time, but equally exercising just once a week will do absolutely nothing for you. The ideal is probably to try to do something active at least three times a week. This pattern also helps to get you into the routine, as the tendency after skipping just one week of visits to the gym is never to bother going again.

As well as exercising and eating at least reasonably

healthily, it is vital that you get enough sleep. And it is this demand which is the hardest to maintain. With the course requirements such as they are, it is often hard to get to bed the right side of midnight. During the closing weeks of my course I became all too well acquainted with the delights of late-night TV: quiz programmes in which you have to name professions starting with 'N' (bizarre entries such as New Age soothsayer always hiding behind the top money squares), cheap sport programmes featuring football from the South African women's second division and horror films. Lots and lots of horror films, typically the Japanese original of the *Ring* and the world's least scary horror film, *Poltergeist*. Finding it hard to settle down to work at the best of times, I would start at maybe six or seven o'clock (having allowed myself at least one hour of relaxation), write up lesson-plans for the following day until gone ten (or often later still) and then start on whatever else needed doing. On an easy night, this might just consist of a bit of assessment, marking and a spot of tea. At other times, there was coursework to fit in – I remember one particularly enjoyable week when I seemed to be up beyond 3 a.m. every night trying to finish off two essays which had been inserted into the course merely because whoever sets the syllabus is a complete bastard. Finally, I would get to bed, in the early hours, but by that stage it's impossible to sleep. The two pies taken as a midnight snack have still to be digested (I never said I followed a healthy diet – do as I say, not do as I did, is the motto for this book) and there's also constant worry about the next day. Worry about the lessons and worry that it will be hard to perform after a little over three hours' sleep (which, I can confirm, it is). Although almost impossible, it is absolutely essential to break the cycle. Try to designate a couple of nights a week as non-work nights or, failing that, at least light work only. A bit of marking, perhaps. This helps to reduce stress and tiredness, and ultimately makes the whole course much more enjoyable. We all need something to look forward to and if your week is spent doing nothing but work depression will quickly set in. Even if it's only the pub quiz, cheap curry night or a trip to the bowling-alley (does anyone not in possession of an ASBO still go bowling? I'm so out of touch these days), try to get out of the house and do something pleasurable (though not pleasurable in the Stan Collymore sense). It also goes without saying that your night off should be finished with an early night in bed; there's no point taking time off work only to spend the time in the pub and clubs of your student town. Do that and you'll need both Chapters 1 and 2 of this book at the same time which, while quite an achievement, is not to be advised.

Taking this time off will also help when it comes to teaching. You should be less tired and will also be less grudging when it comes to work – you have had some fun, so it seems only fair to balance that out by doing some work. And there is no reason why anything need slip. There's a saying about working smarter rather than working harder. Admittedly the saying was probably dreamed up by an American motivational speaker – a guy waving a book around in one hand while advising you to write down one dream for the day each morning – but that's not to say that it doesn't make some sense. The one thing I learnt from the teacher-training course, aside from the fact that there are 9-year-olds who are better at football than me, is that you always need more time for work. You could spend every waking minute of every day working and yet you'd still feel as if you had skimped somewhere. There is simply too much to be fitted in, after all it's possible to spend a solid week working just on an essay without all the accompanying teaching demands. Given that you will have these feelings of guilt and inadequacy, you might as well actually make them slightly deserved. Take a bit of time off, enjoy it and come back to work slightly more refreshed, otherwise you will start to resent the workload and pass this resentment on to teaching as a whole – an association that would be a little worrisome given that you have just committed to spending the rest of your working life in the classroom.

By taking the odd night off, eating well and exercising you can avoid breaking the camel's back. You will still, however, have days when it is only the two matchsticks stuck carefully under your eyelids that keep you from falling straight back to sleep. On one such day, I was due in school at 8 a.m. and so was slightly alarmed to find it was already 8.27 a.m. when I woke up. My wife was entirely to blame for this calamity – her getting up for work at about 5.30 a.m. interrupted my sleep to such an extent that I was too tired to wake at the normal time. (It also didn't help that she forgot to reset the alarm.) But blame was of little use: my wife was gone for the day and besides I had the next 60 years to remind her of the aberration. What was needed was a plan, and the one I came up with – while not one I am particularly proud of – seemed to make perfect sense at the time.

Given that I was reliant on public transport to get to the school and that the next bus wasn't until 9.20 there was no prospect of me being in school any time before 10 a.m. If I were to walk in at that time (an hour after the start of school for the pupils and at least 90 minutes past the time I should have been in) I would probably have been told not to bother coming back. No, it was far safer to ring up pretending to be sick (with the inevitable fake sick-voice) and then, after about 20 minutes of extreme guilt, enjoy a day of catching up. I'm ashamed to say that the catching up I did was with sleep, daytime TV and doughnut-eating rather than schoolwork, but hey, I deserved it, not least because I slaved away at that school, helping out with clubs, marshalling sporting events and yet still didn't get a sniff at the job that came up. (Not that I'm bitter at them and their C of E-only application procedure.)

Learning to Teach while Overtired

Of course, deciding to take a sickie half an hour before the start of school isn't to be advised, but I certainly wouldn't condemn anyone for having the odd day off mid-course if they find that tiredness is becoming too much to cope with. With the workload piling up, it is perhaps better to take a breather rather than to let it all build up to such an extent that the pressure becomes overwhelming. You are on the course to learn how to be a teacher, not to actually *be* a teacher, and as such you owe your placement schools absolutely nothing. They are getting free labour and can cope easily without you for a day, just as they did before you ever stepped through their front door.

Skiving school should, however, be a last resort, unless BBC2 are showing more old reruns of *Miss Marple*. There are numerous other remedies which, allied to rest, recuperation and sleep, will pick you up to such an extent that you are able to go for almost an entire three minutes without yawning or hallucinating that the desk in front of you is actually a king-size bed with clouds for pillows.

One easy tiredness-beating technique is to make sure that the moments prior to sleep are as relaxing as possible. There are numerous ways to relieve tension, many of which are described better in top-shelf magazines, but one that I can suggest in these pages is to have a hot bath. According to some people, this bath should be accompanied by a ritual that in itself seems stressful.

Learning to Teach with a Hangover

(Lighting candles; pouring out bath-salts; finding whales to record so that you can play back their breathing noises; scattering rose petals on the floor.) However, I've always found it enough just to fill the tub with warm water and grab a copy of *Auto Trader* to flick through so that I can get depressed by the thought that 90 per cent of second-hand cars are out of my price-range.

Listening to relaxing music has a similar effect. There's a wonderful scene in the *Shawshank Redemption* where Tim Robbins' character manages to pipe opera through the prison loudspeaker system. The effect on the inmates is instantaneous, as murderers turn into passive recipients of culture and if it can have this effect on men who would kill their own mother for $50 then it should be able to calm a slightly annoyed trainee teacher. If baths and music prove wholly inadequate in relaxing you, then it may be worth keeping a journal of thoughts. Writing down why you feel anxious, and the actions you intend to take, helps to rationalize the thought process and can remove great swathes of stress. It is similar to the technique used by many people suffering from depression – rather than allowing the feelings to dominate, it can be beneficial to try to take control of those feelings, looking at why they emerge and then taking steps to try to reduce them.

Of course, after reams of paperwork, the prospect of making journal entries might be enough to bring on real depression. In that case you may wish to try a glass of wine, a massage or any other little bit of pampering that is entirely pleasurable. It could even be that you need to go out into the fresh air for a stiff walk – a technique that works wonders if my dad is anything to go by, as for years on end he would fall asleep in front of the fire after taking the dog round the block on her nightly walk.

Tied in to reducing stress and anxiety is also a need to cut down on any sort of chemical dependency. It goes without saying that taking illegal drugs can lead to wild mood swings and periods of great lethargy and depression. Just as damaging can be the impact of perfectly legal drugs such as alcohol and caffeine. Alcohol is discussed at length in Chapter 1, but caffeine presents just as potent a problem. The natural tendency is to drink copious quantities of tea and coffee to keep your tired body awake. It's a trait I'm as guilty of as anyone – I'll happily have three cups of tea before 8 a.m. while the rest of my family are the only people in the world to watch *Father Ted* and comment on the fact that Mrs Doyle doesn't brew up with enough frequency. But caffeine is only ever a quick fix, and it is not one which leaves you feeling particularly healthy. My body, rarely anything resembling a temple, turns into some sort of earthquake-simulator when it is deprived of caffeine for any period of time, shaking and lurching like a pensioner on a bouncy castle. It may be perfectly legal, but caffeine has withdrawal symptoms like any drug, so becoming overreliant is only storing up longer-term problems.

Learning to Teach with a Hangover

Another reason to avoid caffeine, or at least only to drink tea and coffee in moderation, is that I don't believe that you ever feel fully awake while you are dependent on the drug to keep you awake. The most extreme example of this is with Pro Plus tables. Pro Plus are tiny white tablets packed full of enough caffeine to keep an elephant awake for a year. Taking one will keep you awake, but you just won't feel very awake. Relying on Pro Plus is the closest any of us will ever get to becoming the living dead – you look awake, you can respond and react (at least on a basic level), but your brain is forever screaming out 'FOR THE LOVE OF GOD, LET ME SLEEP'.

During the day you want to be awake, but you feel asleep; at night, when you want to sleep, you feel awake. Pro Plus plays with your mind – that's what it should say on the packet. My most painful Pro Plus moment came one night as an undergraduate when I had four essays to write by morning (time-keeping never was my strongest suit). At 10 p.m. I took three tablets, by 2 a.m. I had finished my first essay, by 6 a.m. the second, by 11 a.m. the third and by 3.45 p.m. the fourth was done – just in time to get them all in by the 4 p.m. deadline. My marks for those essays came in at 56 per cent for the first, 45 per cent for the second, 40 per cent for the third and 18 per cent for what was an incoherent ramble – this against my overall 2.1 average. I then could not get to sleep for a further 45 hours, even though my brain was thoroughly exhausted. In short, Pro Plus, and to a lesser extent caffeine-rich drinks, will keep you awake enough to work; however the work you produce will be of no value.

Along with Pro Plus, you can file Red Bull. Some people swear by Red bull as a great cure-all, but the only true purpose I've ever found for it is in making vodka taste slightly more bearable. As a product to stave off sleep it has all the negatives of Pro Plus in that it is keeping you awake against your body's better wishes. If you want to emulate a Japanese gameshow by seeing how long you can stay awake, then Red Bull is the product for you; if, however, you want to complete the teacher-training course with any degree of sanity still remaining, it should only be drunk in moderation.

The one overriding truth for treating tiredness is that there is no short-cut or easy fix. If you are placing an overwhelming demand on your body and brain then a tablet or 330 ml drink is not going to suddenly turn you into Mr Motivator (whatever happened to him by the way? I'd like to imagine that he is working at B&Q in Barrow-in-Furness . . .). The advice really is simple and repetitive – eat well, exercise and don't let the work get on top of you. Take breaks as needed, take a day off if necessary and try to ensure that you leave yourself things to look forward to, whether it's a bath, a meal out or a trip to Lake Garda. (Given the choice, I'd choose the third, but we're all different . . .)

Failure to follow this advice will jeopardize your ability

to cope. At best your performance will dip, you'll feel demotivated and stressed, but you'll survive. At worst, the course will either become a chore that you can no longer stomach, or the decision will be taken from you as you'll simply be unable to function at a suitable level to complete the training.

More importantly, you could also do longer-term damage. While on the course, teacher-training seems to be all-encompassing, but step back and you will realize that it is only one aspect of your life and, in the greater scheme of things, simply not worth placing an insupportable burden on yourself for. As with any other illness, if you can't seem to shake the symptoms then it is worth a trip to the doctor. It is not my place to speculate, but tiredness that won't shift could signify any number of problems, including a dietary deficiency, anaemia, depression or even ME: a problem which could see you out of action for several months, if not longer.

Tiredness may not seem that serious a problem, but it can be a sign of something worse. Failure to combat it at an early stage can have severe long-term consequences be they on your health or, more likely, the chances of you enjoying a lengthy career in the teaching profession.

3 Learning to Teach while Broke

However busy you think you might be, there is always time to fit one more thing into your daily routine. That sage piece of advice is something I stumbled across long before I realized that it would be necessary to note down every interesting scrap of information to be regurgitated in a book years later. It might have been a great philosopher that said it; equally it might have been a bloke down the pub; either way it holds true as pretty sound advice.

Take my routine in writing this book. The day starts slightly too late, breakfast takes too long and is accompanied by *Homes under the Hammer* or whatever else happens to be on morning TV on that specific day. The day is broken up by numerous coffee- and food-breaks and I find myself spending far too long browsing the Internet, chatting on messenger, or haemorrhaging money to various gambling sites. During these unintentionally lazy days I could easily fit in several more tasks. I could visit the gym (after all I'm wasting £35 a month on it at a rate of about £70 per visit), the washing up could be tackled, the cat could be fed and I could probably write some of the book. Rather than having time to fit in one more small task, several large ones could be fitted in effortlessly. This reminds me of another analogy (again don't ask me where from, though I'm starting to think that the pub is the most likely source of all these stories). A teacher shows a class a jar full to the top with rocks and asks whether it's possible to squeeze in anything else. They reply that it isn't. (Actually if it's a modern class they probably say 'Derrr, no, of course not. Minger.') The teacher then brings out some rocks – can they fit any more in? No. How about some pebbles? Again, the answer is the same. Then out comes the sand. The class start laughing, or maybe calling little Mickie a thicko for saying that the jar was full. Can anything else be fitted in? Yes, as the teacher demonstrates by pouring in some sand. Surely it's full now? The class certainly think so, but teacher, Mr Smartarse to give him his correct name, proves yet again that they are wrong, proudly displaying a glass of water and pouring it into the jar until it is overflowing.

This is meant to prove two things. Firstly that your day is not half as full as you think it is and plenty more can be crammed in. It also shows the importance of sorting out the most important aspects first, the rocks (to use the teacher's example). If the jar is already full of sand and water then there is no room for a rock or pebble – the stones have to be placed in carefully first, and the other, smaller tasks fit in whenever there's a spare crack to fill.

All of this, while a nice little analogy for how much time we may waste, is useless with regard to the teacher-training course. Learning to teach is all about defying the laws of time, attempting to cram more into a day than is physically possible. You either have to resign yourself to extreme tiredness and a fair amount of stress or, to use the language of an utterly unhelpful self-help guru, find yourself a bigger jar.

At best it will be possible to pour in a bit more sand and water: small tasks such as changing the batteries on the TV remote (not that you'll have time to watch the TV), or nipping to the shop to buy some coffee in an attempt to expand the sides of your jar. What is a certainty is that there simply will not be the hours in the day to fit in anything else major, which would be great were it not necessary for many thousands of people to do just that.

In fairness to the course-leaders and whoever came up with the teacher-training syllabus, they do at least warn you how demanding a course teacher-training is. The application form is so overwhelmingly comprehensive that it instantly confirms the mental link between teaching and sleep-deprivation and the point is rammed home both at interview and at the start of the course. The interview day is an exercise in cramming as much into a day as is possible: numerous different sessions and tasks setting the pattern for the course proper, while the start of the course is full of salutary warnings. Teacher-training, we were told, is the hardest year of your life because you are trying to cram so much into such a short space of time. The job is at least as complex as others which take three, four or even five years to learn, so clearly the rate of progress has to be remarkable. During the day, you are either in school or in college, while the evening is spent preparing lessons or working on a coursework task that should probably have been left out of the syllabus in any case. (Tasks which require you to work out all the possible ways of making the number 20 do seem a tad redundant . . .) Any spare time, as discussed in the previous chapter, should be spent in relaxation, giving your body and mind the chance to recuperate and prepare for the next gruelling day.

It certainly should not be spent doing anything as time-consuming, stressful or regimented as a part-time job, but of course life is not always that simple.

A part-time job is officially regarded on the course as a complete non-starter. Indeed if you were to mention at interview that you were planning to work during the course I would be amazed if you still got offered a place. The course requires the ultimate commitment: you prac-tise teaching, read about teaching, do your coursework and perhaps sleep. You certainly should not be having fun, taking holidays or working at McDonald's for six hours a night. In much the same way as most employers would be unhappy to learn that you are moonlighting for another company, teacher-training is a professional course and places serious demands on you. A course-leader would argue that you are married to the course, taking a mistress is punishable by castration.

And of course there is the training salary to get you through the year. At first glance, getting more than £6,000 seems like a nice bonus for the year, but on examining the figures further it becomes apparent just how unappetizing an appetizer this actually is. It is the breaded calamari with garlic dip of tax-breaks. The train-ing salary is promoted as being entirely tax-free, which it is, but when you consider that you don't pay income tax on the first £5,000 of your earnings in any case, this kindly break actually amounts to a couple of hundred quid at best. It is also an insultingly low figure for the amount of work that you are expected to put in. Given that teacher-training is portrayed as the hardest year of your life, and I have yet to see anything to counter this view, a salary of more than £6,000 should surely be appropriate. If you assume that you work for an average of ten hours per day on the course for six days a week (which sounds like a lot, but is if anything an under-estimate, given how heavy the workload becomes), then the training salary actually works out to somewhere less than £3 an hour for the duration of the course. Essentially, despite having spent three years attaining a degree even prior to the postgrad course, the salary values you at 60 per cent of what someone on minimum wage would earn. Now, I may be greedy, but to me that doesn't seem like much of an incentive at all.

Regardless of whether or not it's a good deal, there is a good chance that it is an amount of money which simply will not sustain your lifestyle. By that I don't mean Gucci bags, trips to Harrods or new plasma TVs. I mean small considerations such as paying the mortgage, paying bills and eating. To cite my own situation: I left a reasonably well-paid job to train to be a teacher and so I had already accumulated a number of bills and payments which simply had to be met each month. Taking home about £600 a month, with no income at all lined up between June and September, would have meant piling up ever more debt and probably having to take out a huge loan just to survive the year.

That is the reality faced by many people on the course: you either have to forgo all dreams of becoming a teacher, or you have to make an additional sacrifice by taking on part-time work. It may not be ideal, but it is preferable to starting your new career with thousands more in debt added to your (no doubt) already substantial student debts and loans. It also seems sensible at least to have a steady income on which you can survive rather than find yourself flat broke halfway through the course with no job or contingency plan in place at the exact moment when the course starts to get really serious with months on end spent in school.

It is absolutely essential to ensure that you never end up in that horrendous situation where lack of funds could either force you to quit the course or place you under so much stress that teacher-training comes to stand for hardship and depression. It would therefore seem sensible to try to work out your finances prior to starting the course. This does not have to be particularly detailed. I am terrible at working out where my money goes – it just seems to disappear somewhere (though I have noticed that the owner of my local now drives a Ferrari). However, you do need to make a list of your essential outgoings – rent, food, travel, bills, for instance, and tally up how much these come to in a typical month. Comparing this figure, which is likely to be significantly higher than £600, with your training salary of £600 at least gives you a starting-point. Oh, and don't try kidding yourself by being totally unrealistic at this stage. If you know that you won't be able to go a year without a drink, buying some new trainers or taking a trip to see mates in some far-flung part of the UK then factor in the cost now. There is no point pretending that you can live the life of the perfect trainee, surviving on £500 a month, only to find after three months that you have no money left and the rent has gone unpaid for eight weeks. If, having carried out this basic bookkeeping, you discover that you will have a surplus each month then you are in the happy position of being able to focus on the course without having any need to take part-time work. What you are doing reading this chapter, I have frankly no idea. Equally, if you have enough in savings to cover the deficit each month or have a partner willing to fund you, then you will also be able to focus on just the two tasks – surviving the course and surviving in school. Rather than having to cope with three workloads, you will only have two, you lucky, lucky person.

For everyone else, there will be a need to generate some funds from somewhere. But, before you look through the small ads, it's worth considering that this somewhere does not have to be from bar work or serving burgers to drunkards in a late-night takeaway. Teacher-training is the only postgraduate course for which the student can apply for a loan, and with the interest rates minimal on these loans they can make an attractive option. There is no need to start repaying the loans until you are in full-time employment, hopefully from September, and even then the monthly payments tend to not be too prohibitive as they are based on your salary which is likely to be in the region of £20,000 as an NQT. At the time of writing, anyone living in London can take out over £6,000 in a loan, while the figure for the rest of Britain is still in excess of £4,000. This maximum figure is based on your existing income and savings and is only available to people who are willing to complete the mother of all application forms. However, as 75 per cent of the loan is non-income assessed, meaning that it is open to anyone doing the course regardless of their savings, income or partner's earnings, it is possible to take out a loan of over £3,000 with the minimum of fuss. This option may be more appealing than taking out the full loan, as the forms pertaining to income are prohibitive, requiring that you list your income, savings, outgoings and the same for your partner, with proof to match. You also have to include details of all dependants and any other sources of income such as commissions or shares. Even if your financial situation is fairly simple, as you will have no real funds during the course and your saving are non-existent, the forms will still use up an amazing amount of both time and patience. Get anything wrong on the form and it will be screwed up, stamped 'Rejected' and sent back to you third-class. At this stage you will have to go through the whole laborious process again, only the delay will mean that your application will now be at the bottom of the pile and your chances of seeing any money the right side of Christmas will be akin to Hull's chances of being named European city of culture.

If you apply for a student loan, and if you are considering it you should get the application in as early as possible to avoid delays in receiving the cash. You will receive the money in three lump sums. It is open to debate as to whether this is preferable to getting it in one go as it makes it harder to justify any necessary large purchases such as a computer, but it does at least ensure that come January and April, when you might otherwise be broke, a tidy grand drops into your bank account. If, like me, 80 per cent of the people you know have April birthdays, the payments come in extremely handy if only to avoid awkward family reunions where you have to explain why you've bought a present from the 24-hour garage round the corner.

With the loan and training salary you will be up to somewhere over ten grand for the year, but even this may not be enough. It may also be that you don't like accumulating debt or, more likely, have already amassed huge debts and don't want to add to that tally. In that case, there is no option but to take a part-time job.

As I have repeated relentlessly, there is almost no spare time in which to fit in anything as demanding as a job. I have stressed this point not because I wish to scaremonger (though I believe that it is a useful tool in selling books), but because it is something which you are unlikely just to take and accept. I certainly didn't initially, but, with the benefit of hindsight, I can assure you that it is all true. That being said, there are still times when your workload is relatively light and it would make sense to try to earn as much cash as possible during these periods, thus reducing the burden when it is practically impossible, and certainly inadvisable, to do anything other than focus on teaching.

Learning to Teach while Broke

At the start of the course, taking a part-time job is probably the last thing on your mind. You have to settle into the course, start on the background reading and get to know your course-mates, be that in the library, in the pub or in the flesh. And it's probably the time when your finances are still holding up and so it doesn't even feel as if you need to bother with a job. Financial hardship is still months away and can be forgotten about for the time being, as can essays, reading and the standards. There is always tomorrow.

The problem is that the start of the course is the best time to take a part-time job. There are only occasional trips to school and these tend to be more for acclimatization than for any actual teaching practice. Away from school, the coursework is, if not easy, at least as easy as it gets. There are a lot of lectures, but the coursework is limited to the occasional essay and even these, in the greater scheme of things, are not that important, as a 40 per cent pass mark is enough to get it ticked off. If you have come straight from an undergraduate degree, the start of the course also acts as a natural continuation of the summer holidays, when hopefully you have been working rather than turning your parents' house into a den of drugs and debauchery, which (I'm told) is the sort of thing that students get up to. Ideally, you may simply be able to carry this employment on, albeit with reduced hours, as the course starts; if not, it at least sets the tone for looking for a different part-time role.

Learning to Teach with a Hangover

Another clear benefit of taking a job as early as possible is that it helps you accumulate funds for later in the course. If you can manage to save a bit of your earnings it may be possible to quit the job later on and focus entirely on the course at a time when it is essential to be performing well both to pass the course and also to stand out as an employable asset.

The other obvious time to work is during the holidays. The Christmas and Easter breaks each last for a couple of weeks, while there are also three half-terms during the year. The course doesn't come to a complete stop during this period: there will be tasks to complete, lessons to plan and books to read, but there is still plenty of spare time. I managed to fit in a week's skiing during the winter break (and very nice it was too, thank you) without suffering any adverse effects, so clearly there is some free time. That said, I did find myself reading teacher-training books while having my post-ski jacuzzi and writing revision notes on the inside of my goggles to ensure I was never completely shut off from the course. Theoretically, with seven weeks' holiday on the course, you could fit in almost two months of full-time work without ever once adversely affecting a day in school or college. You would leave yourself a hefty workload as you would have to combine the day job with any course preparation, but this is no heavier a workload than you experience on the course in any case. (It doesn't make for much of a holiday, though.)

Learning to Teach while Broke

At the start of the course, perhaps up until February when the workload starts to move from being debilitating to unmanageable, you could earn some extra money by working a few weeknights and also for much of the weekend. After that time you should be thinking of ditching the job if at all possible. Rather than spreading the work out so that you do say ten hours a week in part-time employment during the course, it is better to do fifteen or even twenty hours during the first half of the course, saving enough so that you don't have to work at all (apart from the incredible amount of teaching work) in the second half. The teaching and course burden is far from even during the academic year, so there is little point looking to create an even balance in your paid job. I say this from experience, as someone who had no option but to quit his part-time job once the going started to get really heavy. By the time of my second placement from late February onwards my focus had to be on hitting the remaining standards, making the step up from someone teaching the occasional group of lessons to pretty much full-time teaching and passing the coursework. The last part, incidentally, proving to be the hardest, with one essay coming in at an embarrassing 41 per cent (though that did equate to almost 1 per cent per minute spent writing it).

Initially I had intended keeping my part-time job throughout the entire course. I enjoyed the job, which was youth work with teenagers, and felt that as well as providing a bit of cash it helped hone my behaviour-management skills. It seemed reasonable to assume that if I could cope with 16-year-olds who had been in and out of school and came from a rough area, then coping with 8-year-olds in a posh Cheshire suburb would be a cinch. I was wrong, of course: posh kids can be every bit as uncontrollable as those from more humble roots, and also the parents in posh Cheshire suburbs tend to be a problem all of their own, but in any case the job did increase my confidence in class. I also valued it because it was what had initially persuaded me to consider teacher-training – I didn't particularly need the money from the part-time job, but I felt that it might be nice to do something a bit different with my spare time. After six months I realized that I would like to try teacher-training, and the rest, as they say, is history. Against that backdrop it was hard to drop the job later on. I had built up more of a relationship with the teenagers than with the children in my school and felt a certain pang of guilt in leaving. Many of them had become all too accustomed to people leaving them and having spent months finally gaining their trust and respect it was sad to give it up. However, there was simply no choice. Had I not quit I would have either failed the course or quit, as the demands on my time were simply too great. As it was, I would suffer from extreme tiredness and stress as the workload piled up. Attempting to cram in a part-time job could have sent me over the edge.

Learning to Teach while Broke

And we are not talking about a particularly time-consuming job here. My youth work consisted of three hours on Monday and Tuesday, though with travelling and the setting up of equipment it probably came closer to eight hours a week. This may not sound a great deal, but it still had a major effect. Having to leave at 6 p.m. to get to the venue meant that there was no time to fit in any work after college or school, while a return after 10 p.m. only left time for eating and watching the Belgian darts league on Sky Sports 7. Psychologically, it meant that every week got off to a bad start as I was already behind with the workload come Wednesday and was always playing catch-up. While my course-mates were able to make strides with their planning, essays and beer-guts I was Eric the Eel, struggling at the back, taking in great gulps of water and trying desperately to, if not catch up, at least avoid drowning. It would have been a thousand times better to spread the work out. Splitting 20 hours between, for example, Monday, Friday and Saturday, would have had less of a negative impact than taking out the first two days in the working week.

But at least my work was fairly stress-free, which is an essential requirement for any part-time job while on the course. There is already more than enough going on which places physical and emotional demands on you, so any extra work should be of the 'turn up, do as a little as possible and go through the motions' variety. In my case, this consisted of playing pool, playing football and making sure that the lads watching the football didn't cause any trouble. Thinking about it, I wonder why I never went into youth work full time . . . It should also be work that you do not have to worry about. If you feel anxious about your evening's employment then your day in school will be adversely affected and your mood will affect your teaching and be passed on to a class who will become uninterested and irritable.

It would be patronizing to run through a long list of suitable jobs, but the obvious suggestions would be bar work, serving in restaurants or serving in a shop. This sort of work tends to be readily available, so you won't have to spend as long searching for it as you would searching for a teaching post. It also requires only a minimal level of skill or training. I am sure that there are many bar staff who would disagree with that, but unless you are Tom Cruise putting on a show in *Cocktail*, there really isn't all that much to pouring a pint. You put the glass under the tap, turn the tap on (or pull the lever if you're drinking Old Nat's Arse), pass the pint to the customer and take the money. Somewhere, at an underfunded ex-polytechnic, there will be a course in pint-pulling, but for anyone competent enough to train to teach, a couple of hours' on-the-job training should be sufficient to learn the art of serving drinks.

These types of jobs have numerous advantages. They are easily attainable – we would all love a part-time job as a backing singer, football coach or curry-taster, but if

Learning to Teach while Broke

we could do that then teaching might suddenly become slightly less appealing. They also offer a degree of flexibility. One problem with my job was that I always had to work Monday and Tuesday nights and, with essays due on Wednesdays (seemingly every Wednesday once the course had got going) I was forced into doing something I am eminently rubbish at, namely completing work days before it is actually due. It also meant that I was unable to help out at school clubs on those nights, though given that the only clubs open on those nights were junior art (a subject at which the kids were vastly more proficient than I was) and country dancing, this does not fill me with any great regret. It also meant ducking out early from the occasional staff-meetings, but I think the staff welcomed this as it gave some of them the chance to slag off the trainee (which seems to be a popular sport among some teachers). Work in a supermarket and you will have no such problems, as you should be able to change shifts, working more during the weeks when you have a light workload, while doing only minimal hours at other times. Of course, this may not be ideal: you may want an excuse to duck out of staff-meetings or to avoid being drafted into an after-school recital of *Kum ba yah*, *The Musical*, but you can't have everything. Actually, you can: just tell a white lie that you have to go to work and then go home either to catch up with school work or to take a well-deserved night off.

Learning to Teach with a Hangover

Pubs, supermarkets and the like also offer more of an opportunity to cash in while the going is good. Take a job with set hours and you will struggle to make any extra money during the holidays as your employers probably won't have the openings, but work somewhere that is more shift-based and there is every chance that, come the Christmas break, with many of the more permanent staff wanting time off, you can clean up. (Literally, if you work in a pub.)

Having come to the conclusion that the government's generosity won't be enough to sustain you through your teacher-training year and that loans are not the way forward (or that loans alone won't fund your lavish lifestyle), only one more problem exists – actually sourcing a job. For most students, the student union or university jobs service are good places to start; however for trainee teachers these may be places to avoid. Given that trainees receive a salary, and that the course is seen as being particularly demanding, there seems to be a university-wide desire to discourage would-be teachers on the postgraduate courses from taking part-time jobs. Asking whether there are any jobs going won't get you kicked off the course or lead to any repercussions, but it may mean that you have to survive an awkward dressing-down from a pen-pushing jobsworth who feels that you should be dedicating all your time to the course and teaching. You could always point out that they don't know the meaning of stress, that they just sit there giving the same advice off pat to every student who walks through the door and that 90 per cent of students don't even know that their services exist. For a simple life, though, it's probably best just to avoid them altogether.

A better place to start is wherever you fancy employment. Walk into the local bars, pubs, shops, supermarkets and other businesses that you fancy and ask if they need any extra staff. Smaller businesses will probably be able to give you, if not a job, at least an answer on the spot while the larger firms will point you to the information desk for an application form. Given the turnover of staff at the monolithic supermarkets you will be almost guaranteed an interview and will hopefully be offered a job forthwith. (Just don't use words like monolithic or forthwith at the interview, they'll think that you'll be pushing for the top job after two months' employment.) Unlike full-time posts, many part-time jobs can be grabbed simply by being in the right place at the right time. I know people who have got jobs after walking into a shop for a coffee and noticing that there was a small ad asking for temporary help, while another particularly lucky friend got a job in a curry house in a similar way. (And this was after having gone in drunk at 12 p.m. for a takeaway, which shows how discerning they were with regard to choosing their staff – or maybe they just wanted someone that they thought would fit in perfectly with their clientèle.) And it really can be that simple – I would happily place a £5 bet that you could get a part-time job within two hours of arriving in any town centre simply by asking in every shop, bar and café that you come across. The key is motivation – if you really need a job you will do the necessary and put yourself about to find one, if you can survive without one you'll watch *Trisha* and think about all the jobs you could be doing. (That is if you are anything like me.)

A more prosaic way of finding employment is to look through the local paper, any relevant job papers and also job websites such as Monster and totaljobs.com. However, be warned that this method does not necessarily lead to better jobs. You may think that the ring and ring technique (ring it in the paper, then ring the number) gives you more control as you are only looking at jobs that seem reasonably interesting, but I'm not convinced. I've had a few shockers simply because I got too attached to a small ad. Worst of all was the time spent working on a farm. For two weeks, I arrived at 6 a.m. and left at 5 p.m., earning at less than £2.50 an hour (a fact I only discovered at the end of the period when they came to pay me at a rate well below the one which had been advertised. Still, if your employer has a shelf of guns on the wall, it's prudent to not argue the point too much). What was far worse was the actual work. As a hayfever sufferer, working in a cornfield for long periods was ill-advised: my nostrils would get so blocked that when it came to driving the tractor back I was forced to propel seven tonnes forward blindly as I sneezed and snuffled like a man given a tissue made out of pepper. Back on the farm, things only got worse. Because the farmer was a curmudgeonly old git who was unwilling to splash his cash on anything, be that employees or new fencing, a number of sheep would wander into the neighbouring fields each night. With a total border roughly the size of Afghanistan's, this left numerous places from which they could escape. Naturally enough the farmer was keen to source the route of the escape on each occasion, but unfortunately he had no equipment to establish where precisely the electric fence had failed. Except for my hand, that is. I would have to walk round the perimeter, touching the fence to find out where the lapse in electricity had occurred. To anyone watching it must have looked as if I had a defibrillator hidden under my T-shirt. Every few seconds, I would get what felt like a punch to the kidneys, as I touched the fence and felt my heart stop for a micro-second. That job came straight out of the local paper and is the main reason why I for one will never again use that as a source of jobs (the other reason being that I now live 300 miles away).

Of course, you wouldn't even consider a job quite that bad. You will go for something which is both easy and adaptable, steering well clear of any get-rich-quick schemes. In class, we are trying to teach the gospel of hard work, so away from class we should also look for good honest work. There are numerous supposed get-rich-quick schemes, but I have yet to hear of one that actually works – after all, if the people using them really did make millions a year would they need to place an advert at the back of the *Sunday Sport*? Triangle schemes, home mailing, writing short stories for magazines – all of these will at best make only a few pounds and take up your time for no discernible reward. Pyramid schemes may be much worse, as the set-up fee you send off is likely to be the only money which changes hands either way.

If the teacher-training course teaches you anything (apart from the fact that you really should think of alternative verbs to 'teach') it is that there are no short-cuts to success. In school, planning and hard work are essential and the same is true with regard to surviving the course. The old cliché that failing to plan is planning to fail applies equally to what you do prior to the course. Work through your finances and assess whether you will have enough money to survive on and, if not, how you are going to boost your income. A student loan should, in my humble opinion, be the first option as your aim is to shine on the course, not to set yourself an endurance test. However, if you do need to work, try to find something both flexible and stress-free. Find a quiet pub and stand there serving pints to the locals, helping out with answers to the pub quiz and putting the odd tune on the jukebox. If you can get paid for doing that then you are lucky indeed, as it's the sort of experience on which most nights I end up spending good money.

Learning to Teach while Broke

So strike while the iron is hot: stop reading this book and go and do something more useful instead. Go to the shops, the supermarket or the pub and get yourself a job. Then go to the shops, the supermarket or the pub and spend some of your not-yet-earned wages. Just don't tell the course tutors of your plans (they'll only moan), and don't sign up for medical testing. Well, actually, that one is up to you, but personally I'd rather not subject my body to drugs which have only ever been tested on computers (and how much can computers tell you about drugs? – they don't even have veins or a mouth) and animals. That is unless they want volunteers for a trial on the effects of sleep-deprivation. As a trainee teacher that really is money for old rope.

4 Learning to Teach while Coping with other Adults

In life, there are numerous occasions when you would rather not be watched. We all like a bit of privacy while singing in the shower; we would hate to think that we are watched while trying on clothes (though there's a reasonable chance that we are); we don't want a peeping Tom peeping while we read *Auto Trader* on the toilet. But, worse than all of these, is the thought that we are being watched while at work. I have had numerous office jobs and in all of these I would have hated to have someone looking over my shoulder, partly because I would find it hard to perform while working and partly because it would make all those little periods of inactivity incredibly awkward. Fortunately, most people feel like this and so there's a global conspiracy that no one pries too closely into what others are doing, for fear that the prying will be turned in their direction. The only time this happy scenario is broken is when work experience students come in and stare over your computer during the periods that they are not making tea or photo-copying.

But as you have probably already guessed, teaching is very different. In teaching, not only do you have to cope with constant assessment of your performance, you also have to cope with and build workable relationships with a whole host of other adults. Whereas in other jobs you can turn up, sit down, do a bit of work with minimal interaction and then leave, teaching is full of fleeting interactions with other professionals and concerned adults. Forget the saying that no man is an island: no teacher is an island would be more appropriate.

However, there is one person who has a worse deal than the teacher and, unfortunately for you, that person is the trainee teacher. Not only does the trainee have to cope with all the other teachers in the school, the deputy head and head, the cleaners, catering staff and teaching-assistants, the parents and the parent-helpers, they also have to survive, nay thrive, with the class-teacher sitting there assessing their every move. Oh, and there's one more person they have to suffer – the external assessor who comes in for the occasional afternoon yet has the power to pass or fail the trainee. It is a wonder that any trainee survives the whole process at all.

Most of these are fairly fleeting interactions. You can go for weeks without speaking to some of the other teachers, the head and deputy may be 'far too busy' to worry about the trainee, and the parents may rush past you to get to the class's 'real' teacher. The interaction with the class-teacher is entirely different. You will end up seeing so much of them that your partner will get jealous, you will finish each other's sentences and go home smelling of their perfume. It is like having an affair, only with none of the fun. It is hard to over-exaggerate just how important a relationship it is: the class-teacher is far more than someone who just prods and guides you in the right direction, and the quality of placement they create for you will have a huge influence on your early teaching career.

But before we look at what you need from the teacher and how best to form a relationship, it is worth considering how they must see you. Regardless of their character (and they might be the nicest person in the world), they are bound to feel a little put out. There they are, doing a perfectly good job, when a student comes in, possibly to teach their class solidly for three months. The teacher will have had their own plans for the year: lessons they wanted to teach; trips they wanted to organize; and, most importantly of all in this increasingly bureaucratic landscape, exams they wanted the class to pass. Your arrival could jeopardize all of this. If the class end up failing their SATs or other exams it will be the class-teacher's neck on the block, not the trainee's – he or she will have left long since. The fact that it was the trainee teaching for much of the year will make little difference, as the head could rightly ask what the teacher was doing to keep tabs on the quality of teaching. For the class-teacher, the trainee offers only disruption and risk with little discernible reward. They may get to say that they helped a trainee turn into a fully functioning teacher, but I doubt they would get much pleasure from this: after all they teach 30 or more children each year so their input into one trainee is a fairly insignificant triumph.

All this goes to explain why some teachers are such complete arses to the trainee, instantly giving the poor student the impression that they are as welcome as a leper in a Nivea advert. And some don't even bother with the initial niceties – as soon as you meet them you are only too aware that you are in for three months of hell. I still recall the early days of one of my placements with the same sort of horror as the images associated with cracking my head open on my potty as a 2-year-old. The class-teacher must have said two words to me when I entered the classroom, being far too busy chatting to the teaching-assistant about what they had done the night before. And this pattern then continued for the duration of the placement. At best we were civil to each other and got on well enough to ensure that I could at least try to plan semi-effective lessons, but there was no real working relationship. The teacher seemed to relish the chance to let someone else do the teaching and so, far from helping me out, simply sat back and let me drown. Looking back, I don't think that we ever could have become friends or got on particularly well, as the teacher simply did not want me in the classroom. I was regarded in much the same way as an intruder in the house, and was about as welcome. (I was probably lucky not to be shot.) The same could be true in your class: it is possible to go in bright and breezy, keen to learn from the teacher but not to get in the way, and yet be met by complete indifference. Sadly, there is little you can do about this other than to be as friendly and helpful as possible and hope they come round and start seeing you more as an equal and less as a nuisance.

Whatever you do, do not take it personally. It is the teacher who has the problem. Just remember that you are only there for a few months, after that you can move on and forget all about the class-teacher. Taking a positive view, it will also lead to a great celebration. In the same way as we feel great after recovering from a hangover, when you finally remove the itch that is the troublesome teacher it will feel as if a ton weight has been lifted from your shoulders. Go out, celebrate, get drunk and then read Chapter 1 of this book.

Personal relationships are one thing; working ones are quite another. You may not get on with your class-teacher, you may hate their guts for making your life a living hell, but you absolutely have to ensure that they are giving you the experience and tools to turn you into an effective classroom practitioner. The school is paid to have you there and you are owed a duty of care, a duty that should at least extend to ensuring that you get the essentials of a good placement. And yet many students do not get this minimum level of care or any real advice or help from their class-teacher. I know this because on one of my placements I didn't, which put me at a major disadvantage against students who had landed on their feet at the Mary Poppins School for trainees. It also put me behind where I should have been in terms of development which, on a course where there is no slack or time to catch up, is a worrying position to be left in.

This is a common problem for many trainees. It is assumed that you will develop naturally in school, but this is dependent on how much good practice you get to witness. Watch great teaching in all its forms and you cannot fail to develop, as much of that good practice is bound to rub off; watch poor practice and it will be like someone tying an anchor to your ankle then throwing you into the sea. And there are an awful lot of teachers who, from the trainee's perspective, could be classed as anchors.

Against this backdrop it is easy either to sulk, or simply to put it down to experience, get through the practice and hope that things will improve. This is the approach that I took, but I can reveal that it was entirely the wrong one. By sitting back and accepting the second-rate placement rather than really pushing to ensure that I got a great spell in school, I damaged my chances.

One example of this was with assessment. As trainees

we were meant to be getting to grips with our own assessment systems, watching and using the teacher's system. The problem I had was that the class-teacher's assessment system was at best minimalist, and even the assessment that was (grudgingly) done was pretty useless. This was a class full of 5 and 6-year-olds, but the assessment consisted of rudimentary marking of their work-books, using words that there was no chance they could read, let alone understand. If a 5-year-old boy has written 'fgthwe' on the page, is there really much point writing 'a good try, but try to form your letters better next time'. You might as well write any random selection of words that come into your head if the only purpose of the assessment is to show that you have actually looked at the work.

As for more formal assessment, class-lists focusing on literacy or numeracy ability, there was none. Undeniably the class had a great time: they did lots of art, some interesting science, and some of the literacy work went down a storm, but nowhere was there any indication as to what level individual pupils had attained. From the early days of the placement I realized that this would create problems for me, from writing essays on assessment to the more important issue of being able to implement my own assessment strategy, and yet I did little to rectify the problem. I was concerned that by raising the issue I would worsen my relationship with the teacher; after all I was an unwelcome guest in the classroom, so it felt wrong to suggest that they were failing in an important aspect of their job. Equally, going to someone higher in the school to complain about the placement would only have caused ructions and would have meant the teacher having to answer some awkward questions. I was more concerned about not getting the teacher into trouble than I was about ensuring that I got the placement I needed, when in fact I should have taken the opposite view. If the teacher was failing to assess sufficiently then this was their fault and they should have been held accountable. Reporting the problem would not have created problems, it would merely have highlighted an existing one. Would the teacher have liked me for doing this? Of course not, but we already had a relationship that was at best frosty, so I should have done something to justify the ill-feeling.

Another common complaint is that the teacher won't let go of the class. The parents hate letting go of their child's hand at the gate and some teachers find it equally hard to pass the teaching responsibilities on to the trainee. By the end of the second placement, trainees should be teaching almost every lesson, and yet some teachers are unhappy if they are not still in charge of the majority of lessons. Some even argue that the trainee is not yet ready to be teaching more lessons, yet how is it possible to learn in such a short space of time without being forced to do things that you are not quite ready for? At no point on the course does it become particularly easy, as from the very first lesson you feel as if you are slightly out of your depth. However, this is essential experience for the following year when you have complete responsibility for your own class and so will often be out of your depth. If you have have an easy, stress-free placement then the real world of teaching will hit you like a brick. Teaching only occasional lessons in no way prepares you for full-time teaching as there is always time to recuperate between sessions. Real teaching involves doing a lesson, taking a two-minute break, then teaching another, using your lunch-hour to prepare for the next lesson before fitting one more quick session in before home time. And then doing it all again the next day. Getting through this routine as a trainee is incredibly hard, but at least once you have done it you know that you can survive. I can think of nothing worse than getting through the whole year's training yet still being unsure as to whether you can really do the job.

Look upon the teacher as the facilitator of your training, and imagine that you are paying them. If you are not getting the service you need, the only option is to raise the issue with them and, if nothing comes of this, to raise it with your mentor in school or the school head. Don't sit there waiting for things to improve because you will end up sitting there for a very long time.

Rather than you sitting there stewing, that should be the teacher's job (well, without the stewing part, perhaps). While you teach, the teacher has to find something else to do, and usually this is to sit there, possibly doing some marking, but mostly weighing up your teaching practice. At first this is incredibly unnerving, though it does get better. By the end of the course it's just slightly unnerving and very annoying. Having someone watching you the whole time, especially someone who is doing the same job only better (at least they should be better with years of experience) reins in your creativity and your wilder side. During one of my first lessons, I responded to one of the children's questions with a little joke and, while they seemed to appreciate it, the teacher did not. I turned round to see him with his head in his hands in mock mirth at my poor joke. Such an experience is enough to stop you trying a joke again, at least until you get your own class, as being put down in class by the class-teacher is just too demeaning.

After a while you get used to the class-teacher's presence, and can start to relax and perform as if they not there. The teacher is like a particularly juicy zit: at the start their presence plays on your mind and affects your confidence and ability to interact, but you soon forget they are there until a quick glance around reminds you of their existence. Or, to be cruder still, it's a lot like having sex. The first time you have to perform you are nervous and self-conscious, and you get your timing all wrong, but after a while it starts to feel natural and enjoyable, and you turn into, if not Don Juan, at least Don OK. It is a stage that everyone has to get through because the end rewards are worth all the effort. No one wants to remain a virgin forever (at least not in the circles I tended to hang out in) and equally no one on a teacher-training course wants to remain a bad teacher; however, in both cases there is a painful, embarrassing process that has to be gone through to make the transformation from pupa into beautiful butterfly.

After a while, once they are confident that they can leave the class in your hands without it turning into Dante's Inferno, the class-teacher will probably give you more freedom and take less of an active interest in your teaching. They may even leave you alone entirely: one of my class-teachers used the time I was teaching to go and rehearse the school play, though given that every pupil was in lessons I'm not sure how much rehearsing they could do. Perhaps, they were practising the interludes and breaks between scenes, as these were the bits of the play that went most smoothly on the opening night it seems an entirely plausible explanation. With the teacher out of the room, you have both the freedom you crave to teach in your own style but also the pressure of having no back-up should the class start to misbehave, which they almost certainly will at least for the first couple of times you take them on your own. You also have the opportunity to take a slight break, putting on a video or setting a lesson based on solving wordsearches (not that I ever did that sort of thing). But this freedom is only fleeting, for at least once a week – more if you still have a

Learning to Teach while Coping with other Adults

relatively high number of standards to be ticked off –
you will be assessed by the teacher. For one lesson, the
teacher will assess your teaching, looking at how well
planned the lesson was, how it fitted in with longer-term
objectives, and how well executed a lesson it was. At the
end of the lesson you will get some feedback and, if you
are luckier than I was on one placement, you will get a
written report somewhat sooner than a month later
outlining which standards you achieved and which still
require some work. To me, this has always seemed a
most unsatisfactory system: you could teach twenty perfect lessons in a week and yet receive no credit because
the one that was assessed bombed. Again, the key is to
try not to worry about the assessed lessons unduly, the
standards you are trying to achieve never change so it
really does not matter if you make a slow start in hitting
them. As long as you have two or three really good
assessed lessons during the entire duration of the course
you will be fine. Don't try to teach the perfect lesson;
instead, go for something safe that you know works, or
borrow ideas from lessons which received positive feedback in the past. A nice tip is to try to involve the teacher
in the lesson, get them working with a group or specific
child, that way their attention is divided and they will be
far less likely to notice any slight slip-ups. It also shows
that you can plan effectively for the use of other adults.
And, speaking of which . . .

The other adult with whom you will come into regular

contact in school is the humble teaching-assistant. A few years ago, teachers had a classroom to themselves, they could teach what they wanted, when they wanted (within reason). They could go off at a tangent and take an impromptu art lesson on the school field and they could make bad jokes or talk about the football from the night before, safe in the knowledge that only the kids were listening. It must have been bliss. Nowadays, almost every classroom has a teaching-assistant, and it is the teacher's job to work out exactly what they are going to do each day. For the trainee, this can create massive problems: it is hard enough planning your own day and how the lessons will pan out; working out what another adult will be doing and how they should best be utilized is nigh on impossible. It also means that your planning had better be up to scratch: it is one thing bluffing the odd lesson by setting tasks that simply allow the class to sit down, shut up and get on with it, but what exactly is the TA going to do in these sessions? Photocopy? (They'll hardly thank the trainee for setting them such a menial task.) Mark work? (Isn't that the teacher's job?) Put up a display? (How many displays can you have, and does the class-teacher want you taking up their valuable classroom space?)

To be honest (and I have a feeling that I have been too honest in this book, telling stories relating to my potty-training) I never really had a clue what to plan for the TAs. On numerous occasions, I simply set them the task of working with one group and reporting back on their progress. Usually this was the bottom group, simply because once they had started with this group and built up a rapport with them it seemed sensible not to break the link. In one of the schools, I was even encouraged to use one of the TAs only with the lower group. A teacher told me that they would be unable to cope with the standard of work being reached by the top group. Given that this was in a primary school, this was a shocking indictment of the TA's intelligence, and perhaps of the standard of TAs in general, but that is probably the subject of another book and not one I would wish to write. (I don't really want to receive nasty letters from disgruntled TAs – not that that particular TA would be able to write a letter outlining their frustrations.) With so much else to learn, the course tends to skip over the use of TAs; you simply have to play it by ear once you get to school and devise tasks that justify their wages. The problem I found was that I was simply not very proficient at planning in advance. While I could outline lessons reasonably well, thinking about future resources or what preparation needed to be done to mount a display were beyond my simple male brain. As it was, I found myself rushing around photocopying and carrying out other admin tasks long after normal school hours, wishing I had realized these tasks needed doing while I had a TA sitting in the classroom twiddling their thumbs and reading *Harry Potter*.

Learning to Teach with a Hangover

Unlike the teacher, though, the TA has no influence over your success and they won't give any feedback about your teaching unless you expressly ask for it (and even if you do you will probably only get a non-committal 'Yes, it was fine'). Whether they are more forthcoming with feedback away from your prying ears is another matter entirely. Obviously I shouldn't tar all TAs with the same brush (although I can think of a couple whom I would willingly tar with a large brush). I did once catch a couple discussing my performance in the staffroom. The scene went something like this:

Holding a packet of three sandwiches from the garage in one hand and a drink in the other, I push the staffroom door open with my nose.

Inside, one of the TAs from my class is sitting talking to one of the teachers.

They have yet to notice me.

TA says 'He's very different from their normal teacher. You know what he did today, I couldn't believe it. He . . .'

Teacher turns round, sees me, and coughs loudly.

TA has an entirely coincidental change of tack – 'Did you see *Desperate Housewives* last night?'

Learning to Teach while Coping with other Adults

Being a shrewd sort of chap I couldn't help but think that they might have been the relative merits, or more likely shortcomings, of the new trainee. I've become adept at noticing such things ever since walking in on an ex-girlfriend talking to a friend of hers about a personal matter and, to be honest, I'm not quite sure which was the more embarrassing experience. Whatever you do, though, do not let TAs get you down, even if they question your methods or are reluctant to work to your plans. They are but a footnote to your year's training and are at the bottom of a long list of things that are worth worrying about. The teacher's opinion is to be valued as they are actually doing the job to which you aspire, but the TAs? They are doing an easier job with none of the responsibilities and ultimately are there to help the teacher. When you are teaching in paid employment you will have to work out plans for the TA, though they will get to know your style in any case and will probably be able to suggest ways in which they can be of assistance. During the training year, they can be pretty much forgotten about and left to work with a small group or even to take pupils off for individual tutoring or reading.

Sadly, the third person who will come into your classroom in an official capacity cannot be ignored or forgotten about, however hard you might try. The course assessor might only come in a couple of times a year, but then you probably only go to the dentist that often and it's hardly a pleasurable experience. The assessor comes

Learning to Teach with a Hangover

in halfway through the placement to watch you teach, have a look through the files and pass judgement as to whether you are passing or at risk. If you are deemed to be at risk, they will come back at regular intervals, probably weekly, to check your progress and hopefully watch you reach a suitable level. If, on the first visit, they deem you to be satisfactory, that will be it until the end of the placement, when they come in again to dot the *is* and cross the *t*s without even bothering to watch you teach again. It all sounds so simple, so why is quite so stressful? Firstly it is another set of eyes and ears focused solely on your teaching. With the class-teacher also staying in to judge the lesson, you have to perform with two independent judges passing comment on your suitability. There is also the finality of the process. When the class-teacher assesses a lesson it is just one in a series of reports. Screw up, and there is another lesson to put it right next week, possibly sooner. When the assessor watches a lesson that is it. If you teach a bad lesson there is every chance that he or she will stamp the 'at risk' column (or do they stamp your forehead?), meaning that you will be seeing a lot more of them in the coming weeks. The best advice to avoid this scenario is to teach the safest lesson you can, and check out your plans with the teacher to see if they think the lesson will work. Do not try to impress the assessor, as lessons that are overly ambitious can go one of two ways: either superbly, in which case you will still only get marked as satisfactory;

or disastrously, putting you in the 'at risk' category. Safe lessons are just that: they won't win any awards but they will always be satisfactory. Get the lesson over with, placate the assessor and then happily watch them drive off to impose more misery on their next victim.

What the assessor wants to see is that you have learned something during your year's training. Enthusiasm, creativity and your engaging character were what got you onto the course, but these are only one part of becoming a successful teacher. The mechanics of planning the timing of a lesson, differentiating the tasks, controlling behaviour and utilizing the other support available are the parts which are taught on the course, and it is these, far more than your enthusiasm or creativity, which are being judged by the assessor. Like me, you may think that lessons drawn straight out of the national curriculum or Qualifications and Curriculum Authority (QCA) schemes of work are bland, boring and and so overly safe that they are the equivalent to wrapping yourself in bubble-wrap before leaving the house, but assessors do not share this view. To them, or many of them at least, government-prescribed syllabuses are the modern Bible, and every word contained in them should be seen as the truth, the whole truth and nothing but the truth. Depressing as it may be, teach a QCA lesson off pat and it should be more than enough to attain the faint praise that is a 'satisfactory' rating.

Much as I love a good rant, though, it would be

wrong to suggest that all assessors are pen-pushing autocrats. A mere 99 per cent are. It would seem that there are two main types of assessor and you very much want to be lumped with the second type. A few of my lucky colleagues got type two for both placements, a majority got type one for both, while some (including me, fortunately) had one of each. The first type is the one who takes everything in the curriculum literally. It says somewhere, in some throwaway passage, that ICT should be included as often as possible in lessons. This type of assessor takes that and similar edicts to mean that every lesson should include some ICT, even if it has no relevance to the lesson whatsoever. They have a box on their clipboard and they are damned if they are going to let you pass without it being ticked. When this type of assessor watched me, the class was looking at using rhyming endings to spell new words (for instance, using rat to create fat, bat or, in honour of the assessor, prat). The lowest group drew objects that rhymed, attempting to write the words, while the middle and upper groups, with varying degrees of success, created simple poems based on rhymes. At the end of the lesson, a new word went on the board and the class played a shoot-out style game, sticking their hands up before suggesting new words that sounded similar. Overall, it was a successful, if not particularly awe-inspiring, lesson.

And the assessor agreed that it was fine, before adding 'You realize of course that you should have included some ICT. Every lesson should include some ICT if possible.' Her suggestion was that a group – a group of 5-year-olds, this is – could have been sent round the school taking pictures with a digital camera of rhyming objects. That they didn't have the skills to use the camera, or indeed that a camera wasn't available, were entirely irrelevant arguments to her. Fixing her with the look that means 'I am pretending to agree, but secretly I think you are an idiot', I bade her farewell, thanking my lucky stars that I would only ever have to meet her for another 30 minutes for the end-of-placement review. And that is the best way to deal with this type of assessor: secretly pretend to agree with what they are saying, promising to change your teaching accordingly, all the while actually focusing your mind on something completely different. When she was talking to me, I found myself trying to name the line-up from Gillingham's play-off final team from 2000 – a hard task, but one which helped the time pass more quickly.

My second assessor, and I don't know if this feeling is just based on a direct comparison with the first, was an absolute joy. Admittedly it helped that he knew my class-teacher and so was at least as interested in catching up with her as he was in watching me teach; however it was nice to see a human being come through the door. Unlike the first assessor/executioner he came wanting to see me do well, rather than wanting to catch me out. The lesson I taught, while not including any ICT, was a good lesson that encouraged groupwork and led to a high standard of writing. Rather than focus on any slight negatives – not that there were any, if my memory serves me, it was the best lesson I ever taught – he simply told me that I was on the right lines and then had a look at my files.

Unfortunately my files, while being much better organized than they were twelve hours previously, were still a bit of a mess, and the fact that a few lesson-plans were covered in blood from a cut finger probably didn't give the best impression. I knew my folders weren't great; he knew I knew they weren't great; I knew he knew I knew they weren't great; he knew – oh, you get the idea. He didn't really need to say much, and so he didn't – the essentials were all present, it was just the presentation that was a bit lacking. He knew that rather than leave on a negative, thus denting the trainee's confidence, it was better to accentuate the positives. If the trainee can teach a pretty good lesson (best lesson ever, perhaps) then there wasn't much else to be said. Of course, he might just have been keen to avoid the midday traffic rush and so cut the conversation short accordingly, but I like to think there was an unspoken bond between us. He knew that I was satisfactory; I knew that I was satisfactory (don't worry, I'm not doing all the I knew/he knew rubbish again) and so there wasn't much else to be said.

And to give assessors their due, at least they tend to be

fair, or at least consistent. They don't have any vested interests in you and so are merely judging against whatever criteria they see as relevant, be that your ability to teach according to red tape, or just your ability to teach. This is not the case with the final group you will come into regular contact with – namely, parents.

If there is one group that really cannot be generalized it is parents – after all anyone can become a parent. As the great Bill Hicks said, there is no great mystery or miracle to birth, it's just a chemical reaction caused by having sex. And with parenthood being so nonselective, it is safe to assume that there are as many different types of parents as there are types of people: good and bad, motivated and lazy, kind and cruel. For every great parent there is a terrible one, and in teaching you will come across plenty of both, as well as everything in between. By far the worst kind are the ones who simply do not want the trainee to be teaching their child. Their stance is in part understandable: were I a parent, I would probably want a qualified teacher rather than a trainee to be in charge of my child. I would be mortified if, as happens to some children, they had two or three different trainees teaching them for extended spells in as many years. I would find it similar to sending them to the hospital for a major operation only to find a trainee wielding the scalpel. Not that this excuses the sheer rudeness of some parents. On one of my first days in school, a parent marched straight past me to the teacher and said that she was not happy having a trainee teaching her child. She then stormed out without ever once saying a word to me. This was the most extreme example of a fairly prevalent problem where parents simply do not take the trainee seriously. You might be setting the work, marking the homework and having more interaction with the class than the full-time teacher, but in the parents' eyes you remain an outsider. The normal way to deal with this is to fade into the background. (I even took to wearing a shirt that was exactly the same colour as the wallpaper, so that if anyone looked for me they could only see what appeared to be a head floating in mid-air.) I certainly wasn't inclined to try to change the parents' preconceptions: my job was to teach the class and myself, not to worry about these people that I wouldn't see again once the placement was over. And as long as the parents are not openly rude to you they can just be ignored; there is absolutely no point starting a battle you cannot win and worrying unduly about what is only a side issue in your training. It is not as if most teachers have first-class relationships with all the parents – many turn up too much, while others do not turn up at all. At a school I visited for pre-course experience, only seven out of 31 pupils had anyone attend on parents' evening, which sent out a clear message as to just how unimportant their child's education was to those particular parents. At the other end of the scale, the course placed me in the path (picture a rabbit in the path of a juggernaut) of demanding

Learning to Teach while Coping with other Adults

parents who were unhappy if their child did not have homework every night and had not had been heard read individually by the teacher that day. There were times that I was quite happy that many of these parents would only speak to the 'proper' teacher as it took the pressure off me to answer their demands. The trainee already has too many demands placed on their slender shoulders, ranging from completing and passing the coursework to hitting all the standards. Other issues, such as parental involvement and how to encourage greater participation at parent evenings, are matters to be dealt with at a much later date once you are safely ensconced in your first job. Parents do get a mention in the standards folder, but it's a passing mention – one point among dozens. Have any contact with parents whatsoever, and you can hardly avoid them, and the standard will be ticked off, meaning that parents can be virtually ignored (well, the awkward ones at least).

Some parents will go out of their way to introduce themselves and to make you feel welcome at the school. Even small things such as handing the dinner-money to you, or asking a simple question, help make the trainee feel part of the school rather than merely a spare part. Sometimes, though, you have to make a bit of an extra effort. By helping out with rounders, football and PE clubs, and also at a sports-day, I got to speak to parents in a far more informal setting than in the classroom or by the school gates at the end of the day. The conversation was not necessarily about their child, often they were interested in my progress as a trainee, and in a few select cases wanted some betting advice gleaned from my years as a sports reporter. In all instances these chats helped develop an initial rapport that then made it far easier for them to approach me, and me them, with regard to their child. Rather than having to go through the teacher as an intermediary they felt comfortable coming to me directly to ask why the hell I had set such inappropriate homework. And the other parents? Well, they carried on ignoring me and so I ignored them. It was a mutually satisfactory relationship of indifference.

As with so much in a teaching career, dealing with other adults boils down to priorities. There are some relationships which are of prime importance, both in terms of your development and having an enjoyable placement. Key to this is the rapport and understanding you develop with the class-teacher: even if you don't get on you have to get on. Don't allow the teacher to get away with giving you a second-rate placement; by teaching most of the lessons you are lightening his workload, so the least he can do is to respond to your calls for assistance, advice and examples of his documentation. The only other person you absolutely have to impress is the assessor for, along with the teacher, she is the only person who passes comment on your suitability to teach. Impress these two and you will pass the course. It really is as simple as that.

Learning to Teach while Coping with other Adults

Everyone else is very much an afterthought to your placement. The teaching-assistant can be left in charge of a group in the corner or sent off to photocopy or find paper on which to mount a display: the head will remain aloof even if you want to make contact with her. Parents will set the agenda for how good a relationship you have with them: some will blank you and there simply will not be a damn thing you can do about it.

And the final group, perhaps the most important group of all, are the canteen staff. The only time I bothered with this group was on the first day, when I discovered that it was impossible to get a hot meal without ordering one the night before. Apparently, in a school of 250 pupils there wouldn't be one spare hot meal, despite the fact that 25 pupils were off ill. And I really fancied cottage pie as well . . .

Still, if not getting a hot meal one lunch-time is the worst thing that happens to you on placement then you will have been pretty lucky. I got ignored, told that I wasn't welcome and lumbered with an assessor who was more interested in ticking boxes than assessing teaching. I do still hanker for that cottage pie, though.

5 Learning to Teach in an Unwelcoming School

When I die, I hope that I'll miss out on the whole life-flashing-before-my-eyes stage. Not because I haven't lived – anyone who has spent time in towns as glamorous as Maidstone, Swansea, Preston, Crewe and Macclesfield is truly blessed. Equally, while I may not have seen the Pyramids, the Hanging Gardens of Babylon, or lions on the Serengeti, I have seen Andy Hessenthaler score from 30 yards, shaken the hand of former Kent opening batsman Trevor Ward and eaten in the same restaurant as Sylvester Stallone (though he wasn't actually there at the time).

No, the reason I want to avoid the experience of floating out of my body, looking down on myself and seeing flashbacks of all the major moments of my life is because I have a feeling that the whole process will be horribly embarrassing. You see, most of the major moments in my life, at least the ones I can think of now, are tinged with awkwardness and would happily be consigned to the garbage-can of my mind.

There was the time when I was 9 or 10 and went to a fireworks display at some family friends. With no one else in the kitchen apart from me and six adults I had a stark choice – talk to them or pretend to be doing something else. I chose the latter and so spent the next hour staring at the cooker, pretending to be fascinated by its array of (in hindsight) fairly standard buttons.

At secondary school I was never much of a ladies' man; however, there was one girl I was always keen to impress. On the top deck of the bus on the way home I was finally planning to make my move (not that I would have) when a bee flew in through the open front window, buzzing its way straight down the front of my shirt. To the amusement of everyone else on the bus, I was forced to strip in a desperate attempt to avoid getting stung, and in the process angering the bee sufficiently for it to take retribution on my left nipple.

Moving on to university, my abiding memories again centre on two things – girls and embarrassment. Incident number one saw me bring a girl back to my room – a rare occurrence in itself – however, having required numerous pints to garner the courage to sweet-talk her back I found myself wanting nothing better than to purge my body of some of the alcohol. Noticing that I was in no shape for anything other than throwing up or going to sleep, the girl wandered into the communal kitchen, got talking to my best mate and then, only a few minutes later, proceeded to start making love with him. In the room directly above mine. For several hours I could only lie there, feeling sick, listening to my friend and my would-be partner making out a mere eight feet above my head.

The second occasion? No, I really can't go into that.

Thus, at the age of 26, I felt that I had already accumulated all the mental scars it was possible to acquire in one lifetime. But that was before I started the teacher-training course or, to be more precise, went into school as a trainee.

As a trainee arriving in school there are numerous little situations, cliques and even rooms that are heaped with potential problems. Forget the classroom – for the trainee the most stressful moments can happen anywhere in the school. In fact, they can actually arise *even before you arrive in school*. Some placement schools simply don't seem to want the trainee to be there. They are happy for the money and the fact that accommodating trainees gets them Ofsted brownie-points, but as for actually being civil to the trainee – well that is another matter entirely.

The most shocking example of this was relayed by one of my peers. Turning up bright and early on his first day, he went to park in the school car park, carefully avoiding the spaces marked 'head', 'deputy' and 'visitor', before walking into school. Three hours later, having naturally forgotten about parking his car, he was shocked to find the head storm into the classroom, asking whether it was his car parked in one of the bays. After replying that it was, he was told to move it immediately because only staff and authorized visitors were allowed to park in school grounds. This despite the school having more than 30 spaces for a staff of less than 20 people. With only licensed residential parking nearby, the only option was to park in a public car park, thus amassing parking fees of around £20 per week even though there were at least a dozen spaces going begging in the school car park. The school, despite appeals from the trainee, stuck to their guns on the ridiculous policy, and so for the duration of the placement he was forced to pay for the privilege of parking well away from school and made to feel like a third-class citizen.

In this instance, the trainee should have taken more drastic action. Even if the school had lifted the parking ban a clear message had already been sent that he was really not welcome. The chances of a fruitful placement had already been compromised, so it would have made sense simply to start again from scratch. The trainee should have gone to his tutor, or even the course leader, to demand a change of placement. There might have been protestations that changing placements would create problems, or even that it might not be possible, but this would just have been white noise from people on the course who did not want the hassle of finding another school at short notice. It is arguable, and given that they were the ones responsible for finding so poor a placement, the course administrators had a moral obligation to find a better alternative. The temptation on the course is always to suffer in silence: if it's on the first placement, thinking that things will be better in the second placement; or on the second placement that they will be better when you actually have a job. But why should you wait for things to get better? Take action early while you still can, because if you let it fester for a number of weeks it really may be too late to change schools.

While the example of not being allowed to park in school is extreme, many schools have other subtle methods of making the trainee feel like a snowman in a sauna. At one of my placement schools I was never given the code to unlock the front door, meaning that I had to wait for someone to let me in. Given that I was reliant on one of the most bizarre public transport timetables in the world, this meant arriving at the school gates at 7.30 a.m. every morning and then having to wait 30 minutes for anyone else to turn up; whereas I could have been in, preparing myself for the day by drowning copious amounts of black coffee. Similarly, at lunchtime, I would wander out to buy my tuna sandwiches and come back only to face the palaver of ringing the bell and then waiting for a stony-faced teacher to come down and let me know what a pain it was for them to have to leave the warmth of the staffroom to let me in from the rain. Every day I felt like shouting 'Well, tell me the code and you won't have to let me in' – but I didn't. I don't know why the code was such a secret, they could easily have changed it later if they felt security was an issue. However they guarded it more closely than Siegfried and Roy guard the trick of the marauding tiger.

A more common problem is for the trainee to find himself barred from the staffroom. Although he is close to becoming a fully fledged teacher, is doing the same work and should be assimilated into the full life of the school, the trainee is given the impression that while his work is valued, his company is not. One school I looked round made sure that the point was rammed home beyond all doubt, pinning a sign to the staffroom door that read 'Trainees are not to enter the staffroom.' In other schools, though the trainee is not actually banned, the atmosphere is such that you soon realize that it's best to do something else with your lunch-hour, be that wandering round the town, preparing lessons or sitting in the car listening to the radio – that is if you can be bothered walking to the town centre car park.

Even if you are allowed full access to the staffroom, it may not be the best place to spend too much of your time. Staffrooms seem to be full of gossip, idle chat and, in one I visited, scandalously dismissive statements about some of the pupils. I actually found them quite depressing at times. As a teacher I would always want to give each new cohort into my class a fair chance to make a good impression, ignoring any baggage from previous years. Other teachers do not necessarily take this view, and there were many I encountered who were already dreading teaching certain pupils who were slowly making the journey up to their class. It is sad to think that many pupils are set to follow a self-fulfilling prophecy that sees them marked out as trouble-makers from an early age, with the teachers responding to them accordingly and the pupil then playing up to their perceived image. Staying out of the staffroom and avoiding this poisonous gossip may be one of the best ways to avoid falling into this vicious cycle. Are all staffrooms like this? Of course not. Some are jovial places where the last thing people want to talk about is teaching. (If you teach all day, why not talk about something else with your colleagues?) Some, though, have the teaching equivalent of sick-building syndrome: a couple of teachers, well past their best, looking forward to retirement and dreading each new year, dominate the conversation and set an overall tone of doom and depression. When I encountered a staffroom like this I tended to use it for brief breaks, getting a coffee (a regular feature of my days) or wolfing down my lunch. But rather than spend a whole hour in there the trainee can find far better uses for his time: working on getting his files in order, sourcing resources for later lessons or spending some time in the ICT suite to see what software and other equipment is available for future lessons. (At a slight tangent: doing this would have saved one of my lessons from bombing. The class were looking at computer simulations, and so I spent some time at home finding a great site for a future lesson. Acting as a detective, the class would have to solve simple, lighthearted murders – if that's not a contradiction in terms – by working out what straightforward clues meant. I just wish that I had tried the site out in school, because I did not realize that there was a policy of not allowing access to unknown websites. Five minutes into the lesson I was staring in disbelief at fifteen computer screens each with DNS Internet error messages. I'm not quite sure what happened next – I've blocked the memory out. I can only imagine that it was something to rank alongside the embarrassing examples at the start of this chapter.)

However, even if the staffroom may not be the best place to spend your time, being barred or made to feel unwelcome hardly bodes well for a good placement. And there are options for improving the situation, though I'm not going to lie to you and claim that there is a magic wand that can be waved to open the door to the staffroom or to make the school suddenly start to welcome you with open arms. The first option is to raise matters with your class-teacher, another teacher you are friendly with, or even the head. Not that I would expect you to have too much success from this tactic: it is the school, and indeed most probably the head, who has set the policy in the first place, and he is hardly going to renege on an anti-trainee policy just because the trainee doesn't like it. That would be like fox-hunters stopping because of an objection from a fox. And you can hardly complain about the mood in the staffroom, by standing up to say 'Excuse me, people, I'm grateful that you let me in the staffroom, but I really don't appreciate the topics of conversation. Rather than gossiping about the pupils, howabout we focus on something else? Now, did anyone see *Silent Witness* last night?'

As with my colleague's car-parking problem, you could also raise the issue with a course tutor or the course leader. Any school that bans trainees from any facility, let alone the only one where it is possible to have a rest and a cup of tea should not be allowed to have trainees. Indeed, the people who set these sorts of policies should not be allowed anywhere near a caring profession. Be warned, though, that the only practical course of action once you have raised the issue is either to change schools or accept that you will not be allowed in the staffroom. A course tutor may try to contact the school to get them to rescind the policy, but the fact that someone has contacted them on your behalf, forcing a change of policy, will automatically put you in their bad books. You may just find that on your first day in the staffroom you are the sole subject of conversation; rather than gossiping about the misbehaving pupils the teachers will have found a new enemy number one. Before taking this course of action, it is worth considering the overall quality of the placement. If you have struck up a great rapport with the class-teacher then it is worth staying, as it is this relationship which defines your stay. Take it from me, it is far better to have a great relationship with the teacher, even if you are barred from every part of school, than to go in dreading another awkward day spent with someone who clearly does not want you there.

Fortunately, I believe that you can have your cake and eat it. You just have to be a bit belligerent. Simply ignore the ban, or the implied ban, and use the staffroom, entering the lion's den at a fairly quiet time when you know that there is someone you can talk to. Many of the teachers will not agree with the discrimination and will be perfectly happy for you to use the facilities. By talking to them and becoming settled in the room, you will discourage anyone who may enter subsequently and object that you really should not be there. No one wants to look like an idiot in front of a roomful of people, so they will most likely sit there secretly hating you, or leave the room. Either way you have a victory of sorts: it may be a hollow one, meaning only that you can sit in a room and drink cupasoup while people silently stare at you, but in my book that still counts as a victory. In teaching we are, among other things, giving children the tools to fight their own battles and to stand up for themselves. In school, we should be doing the exactly the same thing for ourselves.

The other little private members' club the trainee might find him or herself excluded from is the staff-meeting, though whether this should be a cause for concern is highly debatable. It is probably worth going to at least one staff-meeting during your training, just so that you can see how they function; however, having been to one there is a fair chance that you won't be queuing up to go to any more. In my first placement I had an open invitation to all staff-meetings. I went to two. In my second placement the subject was never broached and so I happily left an hour earlier than the rest of the teachers to get on with some planning at home.

What I saw in my first school was something akin to negotiations between Iran and Iraq, only with a less skilled intermediary acting as peacemaker. Whatever the supposed topic for debate, old rivalries and hostilities would flare up between the key protagonists, while everyone else sat around mentally listing all the more useful things they could be doing with their time. Nothing ever seemed to be decided and, from the trainee's point of view, the whole meeting was entirely irrelevant as the only points raised had no bearing on their time in school. Most of the teachers seemed to regard the weekly staff-meeting equally unenthusiastically: it was something to be suffered rather than embraced as a chance to raise some important points about the running of the school. Whereas being barred from the staff-room in normal circumstances can be taken as a snub and is something worth protesting about, any reluctance to include you in staff-meetings should be welcomed. Trainees can find an infinite number of things to do which constitute a better use of their time: planning, marking work, photocopying, or even heading to the pub for a well-deserved pint. Complain that you feel excluded from staff-meetings and you might just live to regret what you wished for, as you spend an hour each week in a meeting you would happily gouge out your eyes to avoid.

The same can be said for INSET days (previously known as Baker Days, previously known as the day after a school holiday when teachers want to put off seeing the pupils by another 24 hours). Only INSET days probably can't be avoided, as the teachers, quite rightly, will hold the view that if they have to cut short their holiday the least the student can do is to get themselves out of bed and into school for a day of pointless tasks. For that is what INSET days are all about: pointless, time-filling tasks (in fact the letters INSET don't mean In-Service Training, they stand for Inanely Stupid and Exceedingly Tedious). INSET days tend to have a theme, the most common one being the art of killing six hours. One that sticks in my mind focused on ICT. Everyone had to show a lesson-plan that included some provision for ICT, spend some time planning more lessons that involved ICT and have a look at a software package that they hadn't previously used. So far so bad, but the *coup de grâce* came in the form of a video which seemed to have no ICT focus whatsoever (though some teachers do still find the video-player a technological challenge in itself). The video was a form of bizarre Japanese art, odd little shapes morphing together to play out a story. (I think it might have been some sort of forerunner to Pokemon and all that collecting of cards nonsense.) At the end of the video no one was quite sure what they had seen; it was bit like the audience reaction at the end of a David Lynch film. People were unsure whether to clap, laugh, cry or talk pretentiously about the hidden meaning of the shapes going to battle. Did it mean that we are all social chameleons ready to adapt to any circumstance? Did it mean that while we see ourselves as well-rounded, others see us as two-dimensional? Did it mean that we are all dealt the same cards and it is how we play them that matters? Or was it just a bizarre ten-minute cartoon based on an old episode of *Morph*?

Sadly there was little time to debate these life-or-death questions, as we were then set our task – we had five minutes to turn a few random pieces of cut felt into a picture and to tell a story based on our picture. One person made a dragon, someone else recreated the Taj Mahal, I made a stick-man playing football. In a way it was quite amusing – it is not every day you get to pretend that you're a three-year-old again – however, what the point of it all was I have absolutely no idea. It was an exercise in filling time and perhaps a chance for the teacher who sourced the video to show off just how pretentious she could be. And that pretty much sums up the whole of the day; the only useful part was the lunch, which at least served a vital purpose in showing off the catering staff's skill in creating different toppings for baked potatoes. I'm sure not all INSET days are quite so tortuous, it's just that I have yet to talk to anyone who has been on a particularly useful one. The consensus seems to be that they are days to be suffered, and if the staff have to suffer then so too should the trainee. Turn up, go through the motions and aim to get away around lunch-time. That's about the best you can hope for.

Reading the above, it comes to my attention that I am starting to sound like a grumpy old man. To some degree, this is obviously an accurate reflection of my character. I am sure my wife and friends would be happy to tell you just how awkward I can be to live with (or indeed why they decided not to live with me). But I don't want to give the impression that my time in school was spent in the sole pursuit of finding things to gripe about, because that would be wholly inaccurate. I spent at least 10 per cent of my time engaging in school life and finding ways both to use my knowledge and help out in the general running of the school. School clubs are one area in which

Learning to Teach with a Hangover

the trainee can be of valuable assistance, at the same time hitting the standard that relates to showing a commitment to helping out with school life. More importantly than hitting standards, helping with school clubs also offers the trainee a wonderful chance to interact with pupils, teachers and parents in a more lighthearted environment. Not every pupil can thrive in the classroom, so by seeing them in a different scenario you get the chance to watch them succeed in other areas. By praising this success you can increase their confidence in other areas. Praising a boy for playing well for the school football team will boost his self-esteem immeasurably and also make him keen to impress you in other ways, be that in his reading, maths or artwork. Boost someone's ego and they will go from strength to strength; focus on the negatives and you will create an environment of failure.

It always seems a shame to me that some teachers miss the opportunity to share in their pupils' successes. At one school I visited, many of the class-teachers did not take PE – they simply left it to a man who came in two afternoons a week. This meant that the pupils who shone in these lessons, many of whom were towards the bottom academically, had no opportunity to redress the balance with the teacher: all they were doing was impressing a virtual stranger once a week. No primary school teacher could say that they didn't feel comfortable teaching maths and thus leave it to someone else, and so it seems shocking (at least to me), that they can take this attitude to other equally important areas such as music, art and PE.

Helping with clubs also gets your face known more widely around the school. Pupils who previously only pointed and referred to you as the newbie will suddenly know that you help out at the art club, or take rounders training, and so start to treat you with respect and possibly (if you can do a few basic tricks in sport) awe. After helping out at football one evening, I was walking through the school hall when a Year 6 boy said to his mate 'That's the cool teacher who can balance a football on his neck. I wish we had him.' Yes, I'm sad, but that little boost did my own self-esteem no harm whatsoever.

Clubs to me are what school is all about. Government diktats have taken the joy out of teaching; however, they cannot take the joy out of standing on a field on a warm summer's day watching kids engage in a fun game of sport or running their hearts out to qualify for the athletics team. Everyone wants to be there, everyone is having fun and everyone is achieving in an area which they personally value. Whereas the classroom, especially for the inexperienced trainee, may at times be stressful and a hard environment to control, let alone shine in, clubs offer none of these problems. The children want to be there, find it enjoyable and behave accordingly. They also offer valuable hints for effective teaching – if pupils enjoy something they will engage in it and disciplinary problems will be minimized, therefore plan and teach engaging lessons and most of the monkey-business will cease.

Helping out with clubs will also impress the head and could even be a factor in your favour should a job become available. Although as a trainee you will face numerous pressures on your time, attending clubs is well worth the effort as, in what might be a hard placement, it gives you something to really look forward to in school. Although it is tempting to leave school as early as possible to get home to tackle essays, mark books or plan the next session, helping with clubs acts as a nice stress-free break in the day. It is also patently unfair to leave early when other teachers run clubs and in many cases are obliged to organize at least one after-school activity a week. You can hardly complain about the school treating you as an outsider if your own attitude marks you out as being aloof from the overall life of the school.

Not that clubs are all joy, joy, joy, for while many of my happiest memories from the course relate to stress-free afternoons on the school field, there are also some negatives to recount. There is something about sport that brings out the worst in people, especially parents of school pupils. Watching a football match between two teams of 10-year-olds I was shocked to see the amount of abuse coming from the sidelines. Parents were shouting at the referee, shouting at the opposition and, perhaps worst of all, berating their own offspring for slight mistakes. Even as someone who loves football (and made a living on the back of it for a few years) I cannot understand the logic of shouting at your son just because he accidentally passes to the opposition. Maybe it's because the dad was never all that good at football and is trying to live through his child, or maybe it's because footballers can earn £70,000 a week and so dad knows that if he can turn his son into a soccer superstar he will surely reap some of the financial reward. Either way it will only dampen the child's enthusiasm for the sport and possibly drive a wedge between him and his parents. To me, it seems every bit as bad as parents of tennis prodigies who force their child to hit balls for hours a day from the age of 4, and then react in surprise when their cash-cow retires in her early twenties. Still, I did have a chuckle when one such parent, called something like Barry Aggro, chose the wrong ref to berate. Having had enough of the mouth from the sideline, the ref stopped the game and banished the father from the pitch, refusing to restart until he had left. For the rest of the game you could have heard a church mouse whispering, it was that quiet.

Incredibly, it is not always just the parents who forget themselves. At a school rounders match, I was one of the two umpires in a game between the two schools' reserve sides. Both teams were meant to have 30 balls each, and could score a point by someone getting all the way round – one point for getting round in one go, half a point if they did it in stages. Only it didn't quite work like this. The other umpire, in charge of counting the balls and scoring (such tasks being beyond a trainee) gave 26 balls to the away team and 37 balls to the home team (which just happened to be her team). Scoring-wise, her team hit four rounders and got another two people round for a grand total of 12 points; the other team scored seven rounders and got five other people round for a grand total of six points. The posh school with the nice facilities, asphalt rounders pitch and views of the Peak District had won again. They must have been so proud of themselves.

But for all the cheating and parents who either got too involved or not involved enough (like the one who told her son 'I haven't got time for that rubbish' as he handed her his artwork), clubs are the best chance the trainee has to feel as if he is more than some slightly substand-ard free labour. Much of the time in school can feel like a battle, fighting for control of the class, fighting to keep up with the pressures of planning and assessment, per-haps fighting any discrimination you may face and (apologies for the bad link) fighting your own inner demons. And by inner demons I am not talking about major problems such as alcoholism, chronic shyness or an irrational hatred of children, though all of these might be reasons to consider quitting the training. (It must be said, however, that there are some teachers who appar-ently graduated with a combination of these problems.)

Learning to Teach in an Unwelcoming School

No, I mean the small problems, the ones that sneak up on you unannounced, until you find yourself thinking 'Damn, I really can't do this.' Because that is the nature of the placements in school: they are periods of major challenges punctuated by smaller challenges punctuated by the occasional moment of pure pleasure. These small challenges will be different for each and every person on the course. What will terrify one person will be of no concern to another; what one trainee will see as a potential pitfall another will see as a chance to excel. But, whatever your personal hangup, rest assured that almost everyone else on the course has similar worries about another aspect of their placement. I can guarantee that there is no one who finds the months spent in school to be a cakewalk (and where did the expression cakewalk come from – why not biscuitstroll or bunrun?) For many on the primary teacher-training, course numeracy presents an unrivalled horror. Whereas in most subjects you can talk through the examples and then set the class down to a creative task, numeracy requires real understanding from the teacher and the technical expertise to be able to solve follow-up questions. Given that high-achieving Year 6 pupils now regularly do the sort of advanced maths that many trainees never encountered in their entire schooling it is little wonder that it presents a few problems.

I faced a similar challenge in a subject I had never envisaged having any problems with, namely PE. Although

Learning to Teach with a Hangover

never happier than when throwing or kicking a ball around (I often think one of my parents must have been a Labrador), there are aspects of physical education which I had skilfully banished from my mind. Foremost among these was gymnastics. At school I would always make sure I was out of the teacher's gaze, and so might go unnoticed during this most hated of sessions. On the course, and especially in school when I was supposed to be demonstrating moves, this proved to be impossible. For some reason I have never been able to master the simple forward roll. I can do a sideways roll over my shoulder or I can attempt a forward roll and bang my head squarely on the floor. I have never once managed to go straight over unassisted. Until starting the teacher-training course I had never envisaged this being a major problem – adult life does not present many opportunities for trying out gymnastic moves – but there is something about the teacher-training course that brings all your minor inadequacies screaming to the forefront. And so I arrived at school one day having to teach the forward roll, with no idea how it should be taught, how to correct pupils who were getting it wrong, or how to demonstrate one myself. Naturally the lesson was a disaster: seven pupils broke their necks and I vowed never to arrive so underprepared again. (I can now do something approaching a forward roll and might even use it as a celebration should I ever score a suitably spectacular goal in football.) I realized that there really is no substitute for hard work on the teacher-training course and the trainee has no option but to fill in all those little gaps in their knowledge and skill-base which should have been filled the first time around. See it as the Polyfilla effect – you are looking to paper over the cracks as painlessly as possible. The course tutors will help out, holding tests to record progress and providing any extra material necessary to bring the trainee up to speed; however, the only real solution is hard work. Until sufficient knowledge has been acquired, problem areas will continue to undermine the trainee and reduce her or his overall effectiveness as a teacher. Rather than moaning that something can't be taught, it is far better just to get on with learning the subject matter; after all, that is what is expected of the pupils. As a teacher you do not have to be an expert in every area: you simply require a passable knowledge, coupled with the enthusiasm, to make each topic interesting and to enable pupils to achieve at their own individual level. It is not an exercise to show how much smarter you are as a teacher than they are as a pupil.

Actually, did I just say that anything can be learned? At the risk of contradicting myself, there is one thing that cannot be learned, and that is singing. On numerous occasions I sat there in assembly miming the words to some song or other while the more observant pupils stared at me wondering why no noise was coming out of so wide a mouth. On other occasions everyone stared at me, wondering how so horrible a noise could come out of a human body. For I am to singing what Roy Chubby Brown is to feminism, I am not so much tone-deaf as tone-deaf, blind and mute. During one assembly I even noticed that the lyrics to one of the hymns had been changed in my honour. Instead of 'If I had a hammer, I'd hammer in the morning', the children were singing 'If I had a hammer I'd nail Mr Barbuti's mouth shut.' Perturbed by my inability to hold a tune (a failing which became even more evident when I had to try to teach my class a new song for the school play), I sought professional help and, to be fair, the woman I employed gave some sound advice. She said, and I quote, 'For the love of God, never sing again.' And so I haven't. Teaching-assistants can take charge of the singing in any class of mine in future, it will give them something nice to do in between mounds of photocopying.

Obviously, my vocal failings were only a small problem – hardly the sort of thing to screw up an entire placement (I already had a disastrous relationship with the teacher to fill that void). However, they do highlight the sort of small problem which can rear its ugly head and create a few fleeting problems for the unsuspecting trainee. But do such problems really matter? Of course not – have a sense of humour and laugh them off, even make a joke about how bad your singing is, or how terrible you are at art or how you've never been able to catch a ball. Hopefully, by being able to highlight your

Learning to Teach in an Unwelcoming School

own small failings and make light of them, the children will feel a bit less aggrieved about their own personal inadequacies.

There are a hundred and one things on every placement that can't be planned for but which cause a feeling that can range from slight tension to blind panic. In hindsight, much of one of my placements was one big panic. Panic when I was told at five minutes' notice that I would have to deliver an assembly to two classes (I talked about the previous night's TV). Panic when I was given responsibility for half of a PE lesson – I had been left with three footballs and seventeen pupils, half of whom were in the school football team and half of whom had barely ever kicked a football. Somehow the resultant game of dribbling around cones did not turn into too big a riot. And while not panic-inducing, I felt distinctly uneasy, not to say stupid, while helping out with PE at another school. The class had gone swimming and so my role was to stand on the sidelines holding a big, lollipop-like stick, fishing anyone out who might be drowning (an unlikely occurrence in six centimetres of water). What made the whole experience worse was the pedagogic Nazi standing next to me who, spotting that I had turned round for a fraction of a second, proceeded to shout 'DON'T EVER TAKE YOUR EYE OFF THE POOL – SOMEONE COULD DROWN.' Pointing out that they were all standing on the side listening to the instructor did nothing to appease Mrs Jobsworth.

Learning to Teach with a Hangover

All of these little hassles, from being barred access to the staffroom to being made to wield a giant lollipop during swimming, are part of the fabric of a school placement. Each one is a little challenge, but also a story to bore the grandchildren with in years to come. Don't take any of them too seriously because they really do not matter. All you have to do is survive a few months in the school and move on. And always remember that if things get really bad there is usually someone on the course who can pull you out with an oversized lollipop of their own.

Learning to Teach with a Hangover

why we sign up for the most gruelling year of our life by going for teacher training, and that is why many people then seek to make it that bit harder still by doing things which make it hard to concentrate on a course that demands our full concentration. And having taken on a fair few challenges during my own training and observed the (in some cases) calamitous lives of course-mates, I have come to the conclusion that there is actually no limit to how much can be crammed into a trainee's personal life. There are just two caveats: (1) you have to be prepared for a bumpy, emotional ride; and (2) you won't be finishing the year at the top of the class.

Ideally, to get the most out of the training, it is necessary to show a monk-like dedication to learning, cutting yourself off from all other temptations. Sadly, for most of us, our heads are not all that good at ruling over our hearts. One of the main distractions on the course can be the lure of the opposite sex – or the same sex, I don't wish to be prejudiced. The prospect of eternal love or just a one-night stand, can appear from nowhere, instantly taking precedence over the requirement to plan the next session for an unappreciative class. As an engaged man at the start of the course, new relationships (or at least ones I'm willing to admit to in print) were strictly off the menu during the course. My love life consisted of planning a wedding (more of that later) and fulfilling my marital duties, namely reading the paper in bed and filling hot-water bottles for Mrs Barbuti's monthly period. But, as with all married couples, we went through the courting phase.

I have heard it suggested that while on the training course it is advisable to steer clear of fellow trainees, at least as far as sharing bodily fluids goes. In much the same way as many employers now ban workers from dating each other, it is suggested that trainees should remain as distant as ships passing in the night to avoid the potential problems caused by break-ups (and I hope I'm not being mean in pointing out that 99 per cent of relationships started at university end within six months). This, though, assumes three things: (1) that the relationship will not garner any positives for as long as it lasts; (2) that it will break up; and (3) that the break-up will be acrimonious. And even if all these conditions are met, which is unlikely given that most relationships end in indifference rather than real contempt, it still assumes that the ensuing pain is not a price worth paying for the pleasure received. It is simply not possible, nor advisable, to stop living during the course. Put your life on hold for a year and you might just find that it is hard to get it going again, especially given that things are unlikely to get a great deal easier during your first year in school (or subsequent years for that matter).

There are potential pitfalls to starting a new relationship while on the course, be that a relationship with a fellow trainee or someone unconnected to teaching (which might be advisable if you don't want your pillow-talk to be about differentiation or assessment – assessment of your teaching that is). Is that really any different from any relationship, though? Part of the joy of any new partnership is the mix of enthusiasm about the possibilities allied to the fear of the worst happening.

And what is the worst that can happen? Well, judging from the hormonal few on my course who embarked on new relationships it's not all that bad (admittedly that's easy for me to say as I was not the one involved in a crumbling relationship). Although most people on the course were already partnered up, the single few went through the dating ritual that accompanies all student courses before teaming up, seemingly at random. Indeed, looking at some of the pairings it was hard to avoid the impression that they had been put together on the basis of someone pulling names out of a hat – and then redrawing any couples that appeared well matched. Most of these relationships appeared to come and go entirely smoothly. The couple would get together, usually at a club with far too many zs in its name, become attached at the lips for an hour or two, appear inseparable on the course for a couple of weeks and then go their separate ways again. In most cases the pair were not great friends prior to the relationship and so the break-up caused no greater anguish than the occasional slightly embarrassing meeting in the campus canteen. This sort of relationship can be repeated ad nauseam, for in truth it is not really a relationship at all. It is simply

Learning to Teach while Maintaining a Life

fulfilling a physical and perhaps mental need. The teacher-training course is hugely demanding, at times it seems as if your life consists of nothing but teaching, planning and assessment. Against this backdrop it is absolutely essential to let off steam occasionally and this, at least for the younger members of the course, inevitably leads to pubbing, clubbing and then going home either with a kebab or, for the lucky few, a new sexual partner. This new relationship, whether it lasts for a day, a month or even a lifetime, should be viewed as a welcome distraction from the course rather than something that will hamper your progress. It is my personal belief that every trainee needs some extra-curricular activities so that they can come back to the course with renewed vigour and focus after a brief sabbatical. Focus on teaching to the detriment of everything else and, unless you boast Trappist-style dedication, your natural inclination will be to resent the thing which has come to encompass your life. Of course, in saying that I don't mean that everyone should go out on the pull, desperately searching for a distraction from the course, but if you are single and meet someone that you like, why focus unduly on the potential negatives?

Going back many moons to a time when I had my twenties stretching before me, I met my wife-to-be while on a postgraduate course. We were training to be journalists in the love-capital of the North that is Preston. (I have made it an ambition to cram in as many

Learning to Teach with a Hangover

vocational courses as possible in a single lifetime.)
Clearly I had better be careful as to what I say about this
relationship if I want to avoid the fate of John Wayne
Bobbit. Meeting Ali made the course worthwhile: every
day was like spring after we got together and, after our
first kiss, I came back to discover that my room had
spontaneously metamorphosed into a flower-filled
meadow akin to something out of a Disney film. Even if
the relationship hadn't ended in marriage, which I like to
think it was always going to (she would hardly have let
go of so great a catch), it still helped set the course in
context. A good relationship should take priority over
any job or career and so whereas before all worry was
centred on work, the course suddenly becomes an
escape from the emotional roller-coaster of a new relationship and as such instantly more enjoyable. Another
huge positive in starting a relationship, especially one
with a fellow trainee, is that it serves up the opportunity
to talk through any little problems. It is a given that
every trainee teacher faces a fair few anxiety attacks during the year; however, there is rarely anyone with whom
to discuss them. Sharing problems with a course-tutor
takes a great deal of courage; sharing with friends
requires us to unburden our soul to people who probably only want to have a relaxing pint; and sharing with
a non-teaching partner means burdening a loved one
with problems that they cannot fully appreciate. However, date someone on the course and it is more than

likely that they will either experience similar concerns or at least be able to empathize with them and offer rational advice. As well as getting a partner, red-hot love-machine and someone to share the burden of making cups of tea you are also getting a 24-hour emotional support-desk, possibly all for the price of a couple of pints at the student club. Hearing your partner's problems also puts your own in perspective. The teacher-training course can be a lonely place, as you suspect that although other people may say that they are struggling, no one really has it half as bad as you do. Speaking openly to someone else who is also experiencing the extreme work-rate of the course shows that your feelings are entirely normal and that in fact you might even have it easier than some. Don't gloat, however, as that is a sure-fire way to kill the relationship stone dead before it has even begun.

Paradoxically, talking to your partner about the course can improve your time in school at the expense of your time in the bedroom. While discussing concerns (and not just concerns, it is great to share little successes and ideas as well) helps to put the course in context, it is hardly conducive to a passionate relationship. Rather than seeing your partner as a lover you may end up seeing them as a counsellor. Should this happen you may need a different kind of advice; however, for that you're going to need to purchase a new book as I've never claimed to be an expert in relationships. Indeed, prior to meeting

Learning to Teach with a Hangover

Mrs Barbuti, my longest relationship lasted a mere month, and two of those weeks were spent 300 miles apart while on a university holiday. (Oddly enough, those were the two best weeks of a pretty disastrous relationship that cost me a ridiculous amount of money. The lessons I learnt from this were twofold – (1) never start dating a girl in the run-up to Christmas, especially if they turn 21 only two weeks later and (2) never date a girl who wears so much makeup that a Turin Shroud-style impression of her face is left on the pillow every morning.)

My advice, for what it's worth, would be to ensure that you spend enough time with your new partner doing anything but discussing teaching. Plan a day out, do something sporty, take a naughty weekend break or take up painting – it doesn't really matter what you do as long as it gives you a shared interest that doesn't involved the confined four walls of a classroom. And, in the same way as having a partner helps you to talk through the negative aspects of the course, having a shared interest aside from teaching will help to build a more complete and ultimately more interesting relationship.

What to do if the relationship starts turning sour is another matter entirely and requires you to answer some tough questions. Is the potential of the relationship worth fighting for? Will trying to salvage the relationship make it impossible to focus on the course? In ending the relationship will you lose not only a partner but also the only person with whom you can talk openly about the course? And, most importantly, does it feel worth fighting for? If it doesn't then you should probably allow it to peter out, drifting a way like a helium-filled balloon unclasped by a kid at a funfair. If it does feel salvageable then there are a wealth of online resources aimed at providing love-life advice, the only problem is that most of them are bobbins. The first one I came across (entirely for research purposes) promised complete advice, but actually only offered what it termed 'advice for the erectile deficient', and I don't think it was referring to bad builders. (However, it did include the rather wonderful tagline 'it may be his erection, but it's my pride'. Quite.)

Another site required the user to fill in 40 questions about their relationship and then provided a report that was based entirely on the couple's names, using the playground technique (perhaps quite aptly for assessing teachers' relationships) of adding together the numbers relating to the digits until a percentage is reached. For what it's worth, my relationship came out at 68 per cent; more worryingly I discovered that a relationship with my cat would achieve a 98 per cent rating. If only I lived in the southern states of the USA . . .

And however the relationship might turn out, do not let the fear that it could affect your performance on the course make you shy away from ever committing yourself to it. The potential benefits far outweigh any possible negatives. At worst, the relationship will make it hard to concentrate on teaching for a few weeks and may also lead to a few awkward moments on the course. At best, it will help you to remain sane while going through the low points of the course and, of course, a good relationship in itself can be far more rewarding than any career.

While a relationship might be the ultimate distraction from the course (you might even think 'sod this, let's run off to Australia together', and who could really blame you for that when the choice is Bondei Beach or double maths . . .) there are plenty of other ways to disrupt what, let's not forget, is 'the toughest year of your life'.

With much of teaching based on good planning, I decided to test my organizational ability by arranging to get married during the training year. Having so massive an event to arrange certainly helped to take my mind off the course and teaching, though whether it's really wise to schedule life-changing events for the middle of the course is open to debate. In hindsight I was fortunate. With every wedding venue in the UK booked up at least twelve years in advance, anyone planning to get married will obviously have to commit to the event long before they know whether they have a place on the teacher-training course. Indeed, when we set our date, I was still gainfully employed in journalism with absolutely no plans for a career change. As luck would have it, our date was in October, at the start of the course and at the end of a half-term. As such, disruption was limited to the least important time of the course as it is towards the end that you spend whole months in school, scramble to get the remaining standards collected and start the increasingly desperate search for a job. Even so, with most of the arrangements finalized well in advance of the course, the wedding still undoubtedly affected my performance on the course. With an event of that magnitude looming (and it doesn't have to be a wedding, birth of a child, funeral, Bar Mitzvah or any other reason to celebrate or mourn – all exert similar demands), it is hard to concentrate on the course. I still went to all the lectures; I just wasn't really concentrating on them and, while my body may have been in school in the last few days before my nuptials, my mind was somewhere else, rehearsing a speech or wondering what I was going to do if jilted at the altar.

As it turned out, this lack of focus did not really matter. The days in school at this stage were merely to help get acclimatized with the class and the lectures all came with copious amounts of notes that could always be read at a later date. (Not that they were.) Admittedly it was not ideal having my first solid week in school scheduled to start just two days after the wedding. The stress of a first placement is not the perfect backdrop to start married life. A honeymoon to Barbados, it must be said, would offer a much better start. However, I muddled through with no real harm done. That, though, may be the crucial point. Do you really just want to muddle through and fit one of the key moments of your life into an already crammed schedule?

Certainly it is possible to get married or schedule any other major event for the start of the course (and I am not talking about unplannable events such as deaths which we all just have to deal with as well as we can whenever they may occur). And you could even cram a wedding or similar into the end of the course – just don't expect it to be either memorable or enjoyable. Given that weddings cost on average either £12,000 or four major organs donated to medical science, you want to get a decent return for your money. Admittedly you will get some nice new consumer electricals – just today I woke up, had a fruit smoothie, then made a fresh coffee, getting the milk out of the new fridge, drank the coffee from a fancy coffee mug and then ate a toasted sand-wich. And it was all very nice, but in purely economical terms if that was all I desired from the wedding it would have made more sense simply to go on a shopping spree at Comet rather than wine and dine a hundred people just so that they could buy a toaster in return. Weddings and major celebrations should stand out in their own right as days to be cherished and looked back upon; they should not be squeezed into the middle of an already crammed schedule. Had I got married at the end of the course, my teaching would have suffered, the wedding would have become almost a chore as the planning ate into time I needed to dedicate to my new profession and as for the coursework . . . As it is, course-work tends to slip towards the end of the course as it naturally falls to the bottom of a long list of priorities. Add in something as major as a wedding and it is hard to envisage that the course requirements could ever be met.

If you have something as major as a wedding planned for the training year then should you still be contemplating the course? My personal belief would be that something has to give. At the start of the course you could fit both in, but not by the business end. If you already have your wedding or round-the-world trip planned, then serious consideration must be given to deferring your teacher-training – after all we get a fair few years on this earth so there is no real need to try to fit two such major events in at the same time. By spreading them out you will get the full reward and benefit from each; whereas doing them both at the same time will make the event feel like a major waste of several thousand pounds and the course like the millstone that is stopping you from enjoying what should be one of the memorable moments of your life. The only real alternative is to do it the other way round: go ahead with the course and try to reschedule the other aspects of your life. This is likely to prove a somewhat harder task as, while most courses will allow you to defer by a year, and you may not even have reached the stage of applying, other institutions tend to be less charitable. Had I rung up our wedding venue asking to put the date back by a year I'm pretty sure that the response would have been 'Of course, sir, though you realize that your deposit of several thousand pounds is non-refundable . . .'

There is a major difference between putting your life on hold and making the course overly difficult for yourself. Refusing to start a relationship because of fears about the effects on your teaching is putting your life on hold and is a mindset that is hard to recommend to anyone other than those pursuing a Zen-like dedication to becoming the world's best teacher. Life cannot be planned in too much detail and we never know what will happen next. Had I won the Lottery while on the course, would I have just ploughed on? Of course not. I'd have quit the course and gone to live in Australia with my friends and family and become a man of leisure, perhaps running a little surf shack on the beach (even though I can't surf, have the pale white body of other northern Brits and don't even like the beach). On a more likely note, had I failed to pay sufficient attention while running for the train and run straight into the path of car, breaking numerous bones in the process (I'm writing this with *Casualty* on in the background) I would obviously have had to put the course on hold and defer while several nurses (hopefully very good-looking ones) put me gently back together.

Hmmm . . .

Anyway, cold shower over, the point I am making is

that there is a clear difference between reacting to events and actually creating events which make life difficult for yourself. We humans are fairly resourceful creatures and always manage to stumble through when a roadblock is unexpectedly placed in our path. That is not to say, that we should be the ones putting immovable obstacles in our own path.

It is essential to establish what is manageable and what is damaging. It is really a judgement call and so very hard to quantify. Often, it will be little more than gut-feeling that a certain event will be either beneficial or harmful. Timing is everything. After my wedding, it was impossible to take a honeymoon immediately as the following week was to be spent in school. Had we gone away at this stage I would have been worrying about all that I was missing and would have had a lot of catching-up to do. Taking a break might not even have been allowed: the course tutors would have been within their rights to refuse permission, leaving me with a choice of whether to defy their order and get kicked off the course or go to school every day thinking about the money wasted on a honeymoon that never got enjoyed – at least not by me. (I imagine Ali would have happily spent a couple of weeks in the sun on her own.)

A couple of months later, with the course on the Christmas break, taking a holiday presented no such problems and so we jetted off to Austria for a week's skiing. The break, far from damaging my prospects on

Learning to Teach with a Hangover

the course, actually refreshed my mind and meant that I came back far more ready to work. Theoretically, I should have been using the time to get a couple of essays out of the way, but I know only too well that I wouldn't have used the time so productively. I would have got up around lunchtime, enjoyed a day of leisure and then gone to bed, feeling increasingly guilty about the work that wasn't getting done. As it was, I came back energized (except for my shoulder, which had suffered one heavy fall too many) and got on with the essays almost straightaway, finishing them long before I would have done had the entire holiday been spent at home. That my holiday spirit was instantly killed by an INSET day on my first day back in school is neither here nor there. INSET days inevitably turn Mr Happy into Mr Morose.

I had to clear this break with the course leader. I was only missing the last two days of the course, both of which were to be spent in college and thus full of mind-numbing end-of-year type activities, yet it was still worth going through the formalities. Had permission been refused I would simply have taken a couple of sickies, but of course permission wasn't refused and so I got a couple of Brownie points for clearing my absence – Brownie points I would subsequently lose for a variety of reasons . . .

The importance of maintaining an open and honest relationship with the course tutors and leaders cannot be overemphasized. When I trained there were students who had trials and tribulations, as there are on any course. What made the difference in terms of how it impacted on their progress on the course was not the initial severity of the problem, but how they reacted to it and how much information they gave the course leader or their mentor. Some people let their problems grow and grow, always putting on a brave face, until they felt there was no option but to leave the course. Others were honest straightaway, told the tutor that they had problems and a solution was always found.

One student had major problems and found it very hard to focus on the course. Rather than forcing him to make a decision either to carry on regardless or quit, a solution was found. His tutor arranged for him to defer his second placement until the start of the next academic year, which allowed him to sort out his problems and resume the course when he could actually focus on it. This solution had some financial implications, as it delayed the finding of his first teaching job by six months. The alternative, however, would have been failing and retaking the placement (which hardly looks great on a CV) or quitting altogether.

Other students I have spoken to allowed their problems to get the better of them. One felt that her numeracy was a failing and, rather than seek any sort of extra help from the tutor, simply worried herself to a point where it became a huge stumbling-block. Numeracy tests were met with a low score and, feeling that there was no chance of passing the numeracy skills test (a basic requirement for any primary teacher) she simply left, never having had an extra tutorial or talking through her problems. And it would not even have been necessary to ask a tutor for help: every student has different strengths and turning to a numerically gifted friend for help could have filled in any gaps in her knowledge and led to an easy pass. No one wants to be a burden, but if you have a problem you really have to ask for help – these things don't tend to sort themselves out by magic.

It is worth keeping the course informed even if your problem isn't something likely to place your entire teaching future in jeopardy. If, for instance, you do suffer a relationship with a fellow trainee that turns bad and really cannot face seeing them in lectures every day, ask to change groups. The worst that the tutors can say is no, and even if they do, it at least will go some way towards explaining why your coursework or performance in school may start to slip. Obviously no one wants to bare their soul to a relative stranger (especially one in a position of authority on the course), however, you don't need to go into detail. Simply stating that you have a slight problem, outlining the basic details and leaving it at that should be sufficient. In fact, I've always found that it pays to be rather vague, as people tend to assume the worst and don't like to pry any further. It is far easier for them to just cut you some slack, providing any additional support that may be necessary. They have maybe a hundred students to care for and will have seen every kind of problem imaginable; thus they will have ready-made strategies for dealing with most scenarios.

This chapter has been all about making life difficult for yourself. In reality the only way you will make the course difficult is if you place obstacles in your own path or don't bother to inform anyone when you are struggling. Dealing with major events is simple enough – try not to plan any to coincide with the placements and, if you must, muddle through as best as possible. And the other problems, the ones that drop out the blue at the worst time imaginable? Well, don't suffer in silence. You don't have to be a martyr. Tell the course leader or tutor that you are struggling and if the problems do not actually disappear, they will at least become more manageable. I hate clichés, but the saying that a problem shared is a problem halved really does hold some truth in this instance.

The biggest problem you are likely to face on the course is your own attitude. If you are someone who rises to a challenge and is willing to ask for help then there is no such thing as an insurmountable problem. If, on the other hand, you shun all help and allow problems to engulf you then you will face a steady slide either to failure or madness (and at this juncture I'm imagining Jack Nicholson in *The Shining*).

Learning to Teach with a Hangover

At the start of this chapter, I stated that we all like adventure. Perhaps that sense of adventure should be limited on the teacher-training course for it's difficult enough already without extra little challenges being placed in our path. And, if things do go wrong, don't try to be Ray Mears, battling on against the elements. Ray may love to rub sticks together in the Amazonian rain-forest, but we live in a more developed world full of help, support and consumer electronics. I suggest you take advantage of every bit of help available. The ability to ask for help is all that stands between a failing student and one capable of graduating at the top of the class.

7 Learning to Teach with a Mountain of Coursework

If I were king, things would be so different – not least because, as a committed republican, I would have to find a way of bringing down the monarchy. Perhaps I'd engage in as many scandalous activities as possible, though the current royals seem to be doing that quite well without managing to sound their own death knell. However, before working on that hugely ambitious aim I'd make a few more pragmatic changes (and yes I know that the king doesn't have any real power to pass legislation).

I'd make a few selfish changes: the weekend would be extended to three days and holidays would become tax-deductible. Gillingham would get an automatic promotion to the premiership (it's no more than the people of Kent deserve) and all supermarkets would have to turn half their car parks over to leisure facilities. Rather than pretending to give something back to the community with their computer and PE equipment voucher schemes they would actually have to do something that ate into their profits.

Before all that, I would make a change to improve the lot of the trainee teacher. I would remove the requirement for them to pass a coursework element to the training, instead making course-assessment entirely based on their time in school. If they could not teach a decent lesson they would fail; if they could teach and inspire the class and encourage them to learn they would pass. It really would be that simple. Under my system no one would care one iota whether a student could write a passable essay on the changing face of differentiation during the past six governments.

Sadly, with the prospects of my becoming king any time soon standing at slim to none at all (I am currently 57 millionth in line to the throne and I doubt even bird flu will take care of that many people), the coursework element will remain. All I can do is to try to offer some advice to make this burdensome side of the course a bit more bearable.

My problems with the coursework side do not stem from any great loathing of recorded work. My degree was in history and so I should be perfectly capable of writing a decent essay, indeed on many occasions I found it enjoyable to write an essay relating to a key period in European history. In a subject such as history, English or economics, it makes perfect sense to be assessed by

Learning to Teach with a Mountain of Coursework

essays. The learning is entirely academic and theoretical and there is no real practical way of testing knowledge. You can hardly teach someone about Mussolini and then test them by expecting to spend a day imitating Il Duce. When you sign up for a course like that you know that your brain is going to be filled with a lot of knowledge that is of limited use in the wider world. It is little more than an intellectual exercise in dissecting different theories and views, analysing their validity and then coming to a logical conclusion in the essay.

Teaching is entirely different. Learning to teach is vocational. You are learning a skill and so surely the only way to test this learning is in the practical setting of the classroom. Being able to write a passable essay on behaviour-management will be of little consolation if you cannot control a real class that is there in front of you, in the flesh, climbing up the walls and screaming blue murder. Frankly, it is ridiculous. It is a akin to the manager of Real Madrid asking footballers to write an essay on playing football prior to signing them – 'I am sorry, Mr Ronaldo, you may be a genius on the pitch but your essay on how to counter a zonal marking system was poorly structured and unworthy of a Galactico.' In football, you would be judged on your ability on the pitch; in history you would be judged on your ability to write an essay, either for coursework or for an exam. Note that in each of these cases there is one form of assessment and it is suitable for the outcome. In teaching

151

there are two forms of assessment: one in the school which is entirely acceptable, the other which is a bolt-on to the course.

Why the course has two forms of assessment is perhaps of limited interest; it is enough for the trainee to know that the powers-that-be have kindly doubled the methods of failure. However, briefly to set the scene: it would seem that the coursework is an attempt to give teacher-training an academic basis, perhaps to try to make it feel more worthy of being a topic studied at university. Perhaps the people running the course feel a bit hard done by: they see tutors in every other subject traipsing home with box-files full of marking and so, thinking they need to justify their wages, set fairly random tasks for the trainees. Perhaps they feel that they can only justify having a bottle of red wine at home if they have a mountain of marking to work through.

To make it even more laughable (I can say laughable now that I've finished the course, though at the time it was anything but), it is not enough for the course to have competing forms of assessment. Within the coursework side of the assessment there are numerous more little schisms, each eating into the time you should be doing something far more important, such as actually working on becoming a decent teacher. For instance, on the primary course there are tasks for teaching studies, numeracy, literacy, science, ICT and at least a couple more tasks for all the foundation subjects (the government's term for the, in their eyes, less important topics).

With the coursework being so irrelevant, it is easy to think that it simply doesn't matter. Only of course it does matter – not in that it is particularly important in making you a better teacher, I doubt that listing how many printers my school had did much to make me more effective in front of the class – it matters in terms of passing the course. If you were to fail any aspect of the coursework you could fail the entire course and thus never get a teaching job, however natural you might be in front of the class. That to me would seem to be a travesty and yet it is the reality for many trainees who have failed the course and even now must be wondering quite what happened.

On that note it must be time for some good news. It is highly unlikely that you will actually fail the coursework side of teacher-training. Many of the tasks are simply unfailable: they require you to write a list of resources in the classroom, file a lesson-plan that includes the use of ICT, or do a numeracy lesson that differentiates for three different ability groups. These sorts of tasks should be things that you are regularly doing in the classroom anyway, and so you will already have all the evidence you need to fulfil the requirement. On the primary course, you create whole folderfuls of these paper-fillers, each individual task being incredibly straightforward but also annoyingly time-consuming.

Learning to Teach with a Hangover

A few of these tasks are genuinely worthwhile because they help the trainee to think about important teaching issues that might otherwise escape their attention. In literacy, one requirement was to write a short report on teaching pupils who don't have English as their first language. This helped everyone on the course to consider just how they might approach this problem in their own classroom, and also enabled everyone to tick off the relevant standard. Working in rural Cheshire, a teacher is unlikely to come across many pupils who are not from a distinctly white, middle-class background, and so the issue of pupils who don't have English as their first language is only likely to arise fleetingly. For the trainee, this means that he or she is unlikely to get the chance to hit the standard while on placement, so having a task relating to the issue, with all trainees required to watch a video and read texts on the issue was a godsend. (There, I have actually praised the assessment. Just don't expect me to do that again.)

These folder-tasks, so-called because there tend to be a number of tasks which are given in as part of a portfolio of work on a set date, in my case always in a red folder (red folders were on offer in the local newsagent one week), are the easy part of the pointless assessment. There are a lot of them, but they are all fairly easy which I suppose is better than having a few hard tasks which could actually trip you up. The biggest challenge you are likely to face with the portfolio of tasks is to get them in on time. On my course I found that I had four separate folders to submit in as many weeks. Never the most organized of people, for me this was a challenge in itself. For once in my life I found it necessary to plan well in advance – most of the tasks can only be performed in school and so it is patently impossible to knock them off at home the night before the work is due to be handed in. It is worth using the initial visits to school to get as many of these tasks ticked off as possible. On the first few trips to school, the trainee tends to do a lot more observing than actual teaching and can feel like a spare part for some of the time. Rather than fritter all these hours away simply watching the class-teacher in action, make sure that you have acquired every piece of evidence necessary for these tasks. You can even use them as useful practice for later in the course when the workload really ratchets up – if you cannot keep on top of it during the early stages of the course then you really will have problems towards the end.

Presuming that you get the work in on time and you have put in at least a modicum of effort, then you should have little to worry about. These tasks tend to be marked purely on a pass-or-fail basis, often with nothing but a tick acknowledging each piece of work. This can be a little dispiriting. I put in a fair amount of work on some of the tasks, yet the only mark the tutor made was to scribble their initials on the last page, though it does at least mean that you know from the outset that it isn't necessary to strive for perfection when the tutor is often only going to give each piece of work a cursory glance. I imagine that when they are seeing the same task completed by maybe a hundred trainees it can prove quite a challenge to approach each new answer with any degree of relish.

These tasks, while given in as a whole, can also be split into their disparate parts for marking. If one of the elements falls short of the required standard then, rather than fail the body of work, you will instead be informed that you need to resubmit the individual piece that has fallen below par. One of my literacy pieces was not quite up to scratch because I had failed to use the correct referencing system; so rather than getting a big 'F' stamped on the work, I was told that all I needed to do was change the referencing on this one piece of work and then show it to the tutor. There was a real sense that the tutors were desperate to avoid failing anyone and that if any of the work was genuinely below the required standard the trainee would be told exactly what they needed to do and given a reasonable deadline within which to resubmit. It almost felt as if the tutors felt guilty in setting the work and, knowing how heavy a workload the trainee faced, would be happy to receive anything that wasn't basically an insult. As long as you don't give the tutor a piece of work that screams FU they won't be thinking about failing you.

Far more burdensome are the course essays. In my year's teacher-training, I had to write five essays – which is not too far short of the number I would write during a year studying for history – and on that course there was no obligation to plan or assess five lessons a day for 32 children.

These essays tended to focus on an aspect of teaching such as differentiation or assessment. The course would argue that they are useful as they force you to be a reflective teacher, considering a range of differing methods and making a value judgement as to which are the most successful in class. I would argue that the trainee does not require an essay to make them reflective. Your first lesson, when 32 kids give you blank stares before launching into their monkey impressions, is enough to suggest that their teaching needs a bit of work. Any good teacher learns naturally what works for them and what doesn't; they do not suddenly master the class's behaviour by writing a thesis on 'Mind-Friendly Learning'. What makes many of these essays doubly galling is the fact that they come right at the start of the course, thus forcing you to write about things on which you have yet to form an opinion or consider in any great depth.

And they are all-important issues. In the first term, you may have to write essays on topics as weighty as creating a positive learning environment, managing behaviour in the classroom, challenging gifted and able pupils and planning suitable lessons for children with special educational needs. Any good trainee will be able to cope

Learning to Teach with a Hangover

with all of these by the end of the course, indeed they are the sort of topics which turn up regularly in interviews. But at the start of the course? It's like asking a virgin to perform page 247 of the *Kama Sutra*. All I can say is that you should give these essays your best shot and do the necessary reading; just don't expect them to stand the test of time as academic masterpieces. As with the portfolio of tasks, the actual mark you get is largely irrelevant as long as you hit the requisite 40 per cent pass. On my course I was not aware of anyone failing an essay, at least not after being allowed to resubmit, so hopefully failure isn't too much of an issue.

Looking at them positively (at last, you scream) putting effort into the essays will at least get you thinking about some crucial issues and might provide a few germs of ideas to attempt in your teaching. In that regard they do at least serve the purpose of stopping the trainee from becoming too stuck in their ways. On the issue of behaviour management, I had always thought that I would be a teacher who never raised his voice or looked to punish the individual, for example by making them sit out during break. Wider reading for an early essay suggested that this might not be a good idea, as academics and, more importantly, actual practising teachers wrote that a more hard-line approach might actually be more workable. One book I read even suggested that it is unfair to not take a hard line, raising your voice and punishing individuals, as, without this approach, the well-behaved pupils are constantly discouraged by having to work in a noisy classroom and they also lose heart seeing that the poorly behaved go unpunished and naturally start to play up themselves. Having mentioned this in my essay, I then felt more confident in trying out different methods in the classroom. Whereas otherwise I might have felt that I was going back on my principles by changing, or worse still I might have stuck obstinately to my guns, I could now change tack safe in the knowledge that I was backed up by academic thinking. This, though, was a rare example of an essay actually giving me the confidence to change my practice. Most of the time, trainees simply write down what they feel at the time in relation to the issue being discussed and then forget all about the essay (it's especially easy to forget about essays when you don't get them returned for several months). But for this book, I would probably have never bothered to look at them again. What I found when I did was that they were full of statements which were naïve in the extreme. I was having to comment about the main aspects of teaching having never taught more than about five lessons in my whole life. Looking back, they just seem to be a sad waste of time. If the workload was not so bad later on in the course it would make more sense to include the essays at that stage when at least the trainee should be developing her or his own teaching style, having gained the confidence to plan and deliver a passable lesson. That is when the

course-reading than your own opinion. Reading through the essays is the only clue the tutors have as to whether you have splashed out hundreds of pounds on the pre-scribed reading-list (they will have gone from the library long since) and actually bothered to read anything from it. One of my biggest mistakes in an essay was to get ahead of myself and think that it was of more value to write about my ethos as a teacher rather than what I had learnt from the reading-list. I thought that my essay would give an insight into how I would operate; in hind-sight it merely suggested to the tutor that I couldn't be bothered reading through the course-notes or any of the suggested texts. By all means include opinion in your essays, just don't include so much opinion that there is no room to highlight your reading.

Another mistake, one which we have probably all been guilty of at some stage, is to bump up our biblio-graphy with lots of books that, while having impressive titles, have not in any way informed the essay. Scandal-ously, often these books have never even been seen by the trainee, their titles have merely been plucked straight from the university's library search system. If this is the sort of tactic you might be tempted to employ then please take a bit of advice from an essay veteran. Firstly, there is absolutely no need to include a dozen books in the bibliography – four or five books are almost always sufficient if passages from these have been read in depth. And it is also possible to include other sources, newspapers, Internet sites and handouts, as these can all provide invaluable information and, if you do use any of these for the essay, make sure to include them as they all highlight your wider reading.

A better tactic still is to include at least one quote from every book that appears on your bibliography, thus instantly proving that you have read the book (even if your reading was restricted to finding a quotable passage). This also helps show how wider reading has informed your essay. An essay with five or six quotes from different books, tied in with a reasonable amount of your own opinion based on the quotes and reading cannot fail to achieve a pass-mark as you will have hit the criteria necessary to reach 40 per cent. Actually, you will have hit the criteria to reach a significantly higher mark and, if it's well written with a coherent structure, you should probably expect a mark of at least 55 to 60 per cent. A quick word of caution, though: when looking for quotable passages from each book don't simply include the first one you come across, as it looks a bit suspicious if every quote in your essay is taken from the first ten pages of the books referenced; try to find quotes from later on in the book to prove that you have actually read the text and didn't just flick through the introduction.

A final requirement on most courses is to write an essay of your own choosing. Having spent many weeks in school, the trainee is charged with finding an area of their teaching that requires some development and writing an essay on how it needs to improve, what steps will be taken and how their time in school and also wider reading has informed their thinking. This is actually the most valuable piece of coursework as it at least requires the trainee to give some real thought to what they are doing in the classroom. All too often it is possible to notice that aspects of your teaching are letting you down, yet never actually get round to doing anything about this and so the same old failings continue. This essay makes you take a step back and analyse what you are doing wrong and search for viable alternatives. In essence you have a completely blank canvas with this essay and can focus on whatever you wish.

But try not to make the topic too specific or specialized. On placement you may find that keeping to time during PE lessons is a challenge – indeed you may feel that this is your biggest failing in school. (If this is the case what are you doing reading this book?) The problem comes in trying to stretch that out to 2,000 words. There are probably no books on the subject, and at best you might be able to find books focusing on timing in general. It is unlikely to be a topic given much thought in lectures. Your essay will become nothing but your own views and perhaps the views of teachers in your school and will therefore fail both in proving that you have acted reflectively and, more importantly, in being of much actual use to your continual development as a teacher. Rather than writing about an issue that affects maybe five per cent of your total teaching time, try to choose something that is always there, eating away in the background. The big issues such as planning, assessment and differentiation tend to lead to the best essays, as these are areas that you will be subconsciously thinking about every single day. There is also a degree of safety in numbers with these sorts of topics, as you will tend to find a fair few of your fellow trainees have come up with similar titles, and essays can be discussed over a coffee or a pint. It may even be possible to choose a topic similar to a previous essay, allowing you to revisit the assumptions made in that work and draw new conclusions from your additional time spent in school.

Although there may be no requirement to consult with a tutor prior to choosing a topic for the essay, it is probably worth doing so, especially if you are planning an essay on a fairly specialist topic. Most likely they will simply grunt approval and tell you to go and get on with it, but if they do raise any objections you will at least save yourself the agony of researching and writing an essay that the tutor was always going to consider unsuitable.

Having worried you silly by focusing on essays, I should probably point out that there is much more to the course-based side of the course than just continual assessment. Most of the time in college is spent in lectures or tutor-ials, and you will find yourself sitting there, often for hours on end, listening either to a lecturer or a guest-speaker droning on and on. For many of these sessions the best survival mechanism is to find someone interesting to sit next to. Some sessions are well-planned and practical; others seem to rely far too heavily on theoretical learning and providing the trainee with endless handouts copied straight out of weighty textbooks. When faced with a session that simply overloads you with information, it is best to try to remember a few keypoints rather than bothering to learn everything. The main aim of all the lectures is to help you in the classroom, so your real aim should be to pick up snippets of information and ideas that you can try out in the classroom. For example, in teaching studies lectures we were given whole forests-worth of information relating to behaviour-management. Who devised which theory, what methods have been tried in other countries, statistical analysis of different approaches, extracts from hundreds of different texts . . . As material for an essay it was all very useful; as material actually to help you in school it was all but useless. Far more useful were the sessions in the same lecture where trainees got a few minutes to work in small groups, discussing which methods they had tried and found to be effective. All the psychobabble went in one ear and straight out the other.

The teaching studies sessions are probably the most useful of all the lectures. Whereas other sessions focus on what you will be teaching, teaching studies looks at the actual mechanics of doing the job. The subject matter is all stuff that can be learned simply by putting the time in to do the reading. The lectures tend to give you pointers and maybe practical examples of lessons, but the real work has to be done by the trainee. If you find that the timetable requires you to teach a topic you know nothing about, there is simply no option but to go the library and carry out the requisite reading to enhance your knowledge. This knowledge will not be gained by going to any number of lectures, as it is neither practical, nor indeed possible, for the tutor to teach every topic on the syllabus. Instead, they can only work through a few examples and encourage the trainee to put in the extra effort. And, if the reading is done, there is no topic that should prove to be unteachable: after all, the mechanics of setting objectives and teaching an engaging lesson remain the same.

Teaching studies deals with the intangibles, the things that have to click into place and cannot simply be picked up by any amount of reading. The trainee could read a thousand books on planning good lessons, but until they have actually planned a good lesson of their own all this is irrelevant. It is the confidence that comes from having succeeded that enables progress to be made and a pattern set that can be repeated in future lessons. Teaching studies, at least the more useful parts of these sessions, forces the trainee to think about their own teaching and to accept that they will have to try different methods in the classroom. Hopefully it also instils confidence in the trainee to risk new approaches that might not actually work. In striving for excellence, it is far better to teach the odd dodgy lesson than to accept a level of mediocrity that leads to a quiet but uninspired class.

When attending teaching studies lectures, take nothing for granted. You will have your own preconceived ideas, but don't allow these to cut off all other possibilities. Go in with an open mind and be willing to try out any new methods that are suggested. If they don't work then maybe that simply confirms that you were right in your initial thinking. (Smart arse.)

And for all the learning that you will have to do on the course, try to enjoy the lectures as they are the downtime in a hectic year. Although a three-hour lecture on English theory may not be everyone's cup of tea, you are at least getting to mingle with your peers and can always pop to the pub afterwards for a chat about what you have learned. Or for a pint to help you forget. And during the lectures I had constantly to remind myself just how lucky I was to be there – not because thousands of people apply and don't get on the course, but because it is so much better than sitting in an office doing a soulless nine to five. Much of the time in lectures is spent carrying out tasks that should appeal to the class, so the trainees are getting to experience school all over again. Given that school years are regularly portrayed as the best years of your life, this cannot be a bad thing. At times when I could easily have been writing a report, sitting in a meeting or doing some filing in another job, I was instead in a drama session, pretending to be pushing a boulder; in a music session, composing a tune out of home-made percussion instruments; or in a numeracy session, playing a number game. Admittedly, the last one might not sound appealing, but I'm something of a geek when it comes to maths tests. (Think you can beat me on mental arithmetic? What's 12 squared? 144. There, I beat you!)

Worry a bit about the essays and other tasks, but don't worry too much. As long as you don't take the mick and do at least some of the suggested wider reading you should walk these tasks. Unlike on a more academic course, the tutors have no real interest in seeking to fail any of the students; instead they just want to see that they are considering the issues that impact on their teaching.

And although I've been highly critical of the course assessment, it is probably a reasonable aim. The tutors won't be placing too much emphasis on your writing, they will be looking at whether you are thinking about what necessary steps need to be taken to become a top-class teacher. And, regardless of any essay requirements, this is something you should already be doing off your own bat.

8 Home-time

While researching this book – research in this case being getting drunk for Chapter 1, staying up late for Chapter 2, living beyond my means for Chapter 3 – you get the idea – I came up with a few little pieces of information which, while useful, didn't seem to fit into any of the main chapters. So I offer them here, in what I hope is a helpful and satisfying conclusion.

One of the most important pieces of advice I can offer is to value the friendships you make on the course. At the start of our year, we were told that the friends we made on the course would be our friends for life and that they would quickly supersede our existing chums. Statements like this tend to be met with a degree of scorn: personally I felt that I already had more than enough friends – too many birthdays to forget – and was on the course to learn how to teach, not to acquire new drinking buddies. (Not that new drinking buddies aren't always welcome.)

Learning to Teach with a Hangover

And a couple of weeks into the course I was even less convinced by the validity of the claim – the most interesting conversation I had engaged in with any other trainee concerned Crewe town centre, while most trainees seemed to simply turn up and then go home as soon as the lectures were over. With mingling at an all-time low for a student course, the chances of making any contacts let alone genuine friends were similar to Paul Gascoigne's chances of ever being asked to guest-present *Question Time*.

Yet as the workload picked up, this slowly changed. Rather than rushing straight home, people seemed far keener to stay behind, either in the library, the canteen or the pub, and have some human contact. Whereas the start of the training is relatively easy, as it is just a case of turning up at lectures, the increased workload made it far more necessary for everyone to start turning to their fellow trainees for help and advice. Naturally, this can't be done out the blue – you can hardly go up to someone you have never spoken to and ask them for their opinions on a key part of the course. Instead, everyone starts slowly to build relationships, perhaps subconsciously creating the support group that they will later come to rely upon.

Having had acquaintances but no real friends on the course after a couple of weeks (which sounds a bit tragic now I've actually written it down), within a month I had what I would consider good mates. That's the nature of student courses: because you are in constant contact with people things can change very quickly and relationships grow and crumble at an amazing rate. Watching a student course from the outside must be like watching a plant grow and die using that accelerated camera beloved by BBC natural history programmes.

Initially these friendships were based on anything but teaching. They were formed on the course, but we rarely talked about teaching matters. If we had just talked about teaching it wouldn't have been much of a friendship – it would simply have been a relationship of convenience. Over time, as we all had our own issues on the course, the focus was much more on teaching. Having friends to turn to meant we could each raise our concerns over a pint knowing that we would either get a friendly piece of advice or be told to stop being so stupid. And as two people rarely experience their lows at exactly the same time, we could always be sure to receive advice from a friend who had a more stable state of mind. Rather than simply stewing on our problems, they were put into perspective over a pint and game of pub *Who Wants to be a Millionaire?*

The value of good friendships on the course simply cannot be overstated. The people you become close to on the course may not become lifelong friends – very few people fall into that category. However, for the time you are on the course and during your first year or two in teaching they will prove to be more useful than any other friend you already have. They will be the ones to whom you can turn over any issue relating to your profession and from whom you can expect to get sound advice. Whereas non-teaching friends would only be able to offer a sympathetic ear, your course-mates can offer a sympathetic ear and some practical advice.

Unfortunately, these great mates don't just appear one day. Making friends requires work as it is only by taking the time to get to know people that they turn from being someone to grunt good morning to to someone you could actually ring up and ask to meet up with. At the start of the course you have to take the time to meet fellow trainees away from the lecture hall, be it to have lunch in the canteen, go looking for books in the library or to play pool or go and check out the local shops. All this socializing can be nerve-wracking initially, but it is worth remembering that most people are in the same position and don't really know anyone else on the course. There will be almost no one on the course who wouldn't welcome a bit of company and a chat about teaching or something more frivolous. And the friends you make at the start of the course do not have to be bosom buddies. Get to know a few people and from them your social circle will grow and you will be able to pick and choose the useful and interesting friends, like the socialite you are, and discard the rest like sand from a sandal.

Whether all friends are quite so useful is debatable. We all love our extrovert mates who go out seven days a week and are the life and soul of every party. However, these friends tend either to be holding down a job at Asda or doing a course which requires minimal attendance or commitment. History, for example. These friends will almost certainly not be on a teacher-training course and so they are unlikely to realize just how pressed you will be for time and just how little time you can dedicate to hedonism. If you are on a postgraduate teaching course, it is seriously worth considering who you live with. The chances are that you will have made friends already and will be considering living with people you shared with during your undergraduate studies. This though could spell disaster. While their life might still consist of going out every night and hosting impromptu parties at home, yours will have to be turned over to the pleasures of reading and planning. Sadly it will not be possible to concentrate on the course – and concentration really is essential if you are going to pass – with your housemates partying or making a lot of noise every night. For the sake of your future career, it may be well worth considering only living with other postgrads or young professionals who will face similar demands and be more understanding towards your pleas for quiet. Continuing to live with people with a more leisurely lifestyle is only likely to lead to strained relationships and previously strong friendships disintegrating under accusations that either you have changed or your former friends are selfishly ignoring your needs.

Learning to Teach with a Hangover

By separating yourself from people more inclined to party every night you will actually value the time you spend with them more. You can always arrange to meet up for a night out: after all it is essential to let off steam during the course. However, this letting off steam should be on your terms, as being forced to suffer a chaotic atmosphere when all you want to do is work will only increase your own stress levels. You will end up letting off steam, only the release of tension will be aimed solely at your housemates.

Even if you have a perfectly quiet house, the question remains what should you be doing in it? By the end of the course, the workload takes care of itself. A trainee in final placement feels like a man with a leaking boat stuck in the middle of the Atlantic Ocean – it is all they can do to keep bailing out, keeping their head above water. All instincts are tuned to survival and so there is no option but to plough on with the relentless work schedule. Yet at the start of the course this isn't the case.

It is entirely likely that you won't have any work to hand in for the first couple of months of the course and the time in school will consist of a lot more observing than actual teaching. It is all too easy to fall into a pattern at this stage, enjoying what seems to be an easy start to the course and kidding yourself that you can always pick up the workload later on. Only it really is not that simple. The workload suddenly rises like a tsunami and, where once no imminent deadlines loomed, suddenly several pieces of coursework will coincide with your first full day of teaching or your first lengthy spell in school. I was as guilty as anyone in enjoying the lull at the start of the course, so I can only offer advice that, with hindsight, I wish I had taken. Work hard at the start of the course and, at the very least, work through some of the wider reading, making notes to inform some of the essays. Better still, get a couple of essays knocked off long before the deadline and complete as many tasks as possible on your initial visits to school. Having established a pattern of work it will become far easier to maintain it, rather than trying to go straight from neutral to fifth gear a few months in. An additional bonus of knocking tasks off early is that you might actually find that a few of the suggested books are still in the library. Leave it too late and every book on the list will have gone, along with every book with a similar sounding title. It's a position I have found myself in on many occasions, desperately leafing through the empty shelves where the books I need should be stored, trying to find a title that appears to have at least some semblance of relevance and a quotable passage or two. Once or twice on the teaching course it got so bad that I would find myself writing an essay the night before it was due in with only a couple of books, and largely irrelevant books at that, to guide my thinking. At these junctures I turned to the Amazon website: obviously it was too late to order a book; however, their browse facility proved invaluable. Many books on the site include a chapter of sample text and so by entering a few titles from the reading-list I was eventually able to find a couple that included excerpts from relevant chapters. While perhaps not enough for a really informed essay, these did at least provide a few useful lines to quote. Not that I would recommend this approach: it was stressful and actually took far longer than simply reading through the book. It would have made more sense to have at least sourced the books a while before writing the essay, even if the actual writing did still take until 4 a.m. on the deadline morning.

But that is enough about problems. Most of all you should just try to enjoy the course. When the workload gets too much, or when you have to go into school with a raging hangover it can be easy to forget the moments of elation. But remember how good it felt when you found out that you were accepted onto the course. Tens of thousands of people apply every year; only a small percentage actually make it. Try to remember that you are one of the lucky ones and that you have been granted an amazing opportunity to change people's lives for the better by inspiring them to a life full of learning.

There will be low points on the course, but my aim in this book has been to show you that they are only temporary stumbling-blocks and that you are by no means alone in experiencing the odd difficulty. When you were applying for the course, no one ever said that it would be easy. However, they did promise that the hard work would be worth it, and they were right.

Teaching can be a deeply fulfilling career. It is also a most important career, as you will influence thousands of lives during your time as a teacher. Everyone you teach deserves the highest standard of education and so the course has to be hard to ensure that you hit the high standards demanded. But, however tough it may get, never despair. When you see your pupils actively engaging in your lesson, or when, years later, past pupils thank you for being such a great teacher, you will know that all the hard work was well worth it. A moment's pain for a lifetime's reward: that to me sounds like a price worth paying.

Further Reading

On the teacher training course there are dozens of reading lists to be negotiated or ignored, depending on your dedication to the course. But most of these lists are of limited use as the books are often pitched at far too high a level for the inexperienced trainee.

What would be far more useful is a reading list designed to help you pass the course and to work through the myriad problems that will inevitably occur. The reading lists offering advanced insight into teaching theory can probably wait.

And so, without further ado, here is just such a list. I just wish someone had bothered making one a couple of years ago . . .

Allen, David, *Getting Things Done: The Art of Stress-free Productivity* (London: Piatkus, 2002). This book is a godsend for the trainee. The two main problems are stress and time-management – time-management meaning trying to squeeze an extra seven tasks into an already crammed schedule. This book tackles both areas, giving advice on how you can get more done and remain relatively stress-free at the same time. If it sounds too good to be true, this is because, to some extent, it is. However, there are enough little gems in here to make it well worth a loan from the library.

Barbuti, Jon, *The Inside Guide to Training as a Teacher* (London: Continuum, 2006). Putting my own book in my own reading list – is that sensible or shameless? Personally, I'd say it's an unselfish act aimed at helping out trainees for, if you buy just one book this year, it should be this one. If you can afford two books, buy this one twice. This book acts as a diary to my time on the course, following the ups and downs of a PGCE student.

Baxendale, Martin, *The Hangover Survival Guide* (UK: Silent But Deadly Publications, 2005). It's only about 30 pages long, but with a hangover that's probably about all you can cope with. Although much of the book is in cartoon form, there are some useful snippets of advice. And better still, it is dirt cheap and so doesn't impinge on your ability to buy more pints.

Bennett, Hazel, *Trainee Teacher's Survival Guide* (London: Continuum, 2006). This is the sort of book I wish I'd had while training to teach. It might not be as good as *The*

Inside Guide to Training as a Teacher, but it's still a near-essential for any trainee. This book is full of detail and for anyone worrying about the standards, this is the text for them.

Bourne, Edmund, *The Anxiety and Phobia Workbook* (Oakland, CA: New Harbinger, 2005). Teacher training is a stressful time. During my year I had numerous little panic attacks, usually at about 8.30 a.m. as it suddenly dawned on me that the lesson I had planned was doomed to bomb. This book is the most effective I have come across for tackling stress and that's coming from someone who generally hates American self-help books.

Cowley, Sue, *Guerrilla Guide to Teaching* (London: Continuum, 2002). Sue Cowley's books offer heaps of practical hints and tips to teachers of all levels of experience. This book has yet more practical tips. I don't know where she gets them all from, to be honest – you get the impression she could write a book a week full of a new set of teaching aids. Incredible stuff.

Cowley, Sue, *Getting the Buggers to Behave* (London: Continuum, 2006). I hope Sue offers me commission, because this is her second mention in my reading-list. For my money, this is the most useful book in the series, but there are many other 'Getting the Buggers to . . .' books that are worth a look. I believe the next book in

Further Reading

the series is *Getting the Buggers to Stop Copying their Teacher's Swearing*.

Ford, Norman, *Eighteen Natural Ways to Beat Chronic Tiredness* (Newhaven, CT: Keats, 1994). I saw this book in the library and was impressed with some of the tips on beating tiredness. The fact that the remedies are natural also appeals – after all I don't want to recommend an approach that sees you getting hooked on Pro Plus.

Hill, Eric, *Where's Spot?* (London: Puffin Books, 2003). The first book I read in Manchester Metropolitan University's library (all the proper books had been taken out). A seminal classic that sees an increasingly exacerbated Sally search for her errant son.

Overall, Lyn and Sangster, Margaret, *Primary Teacher's Handbook* (London: Continuum, 2006). Any book containing the word handbook in the title should be fairly dry, but also reassuringly authoritative. This doesn't disappoint.

Scrivner, Jane, *The Quick-fix Hangover Detox: 99 Ways to Feel 100 Times Better* (London: Piatkus, 2001). It strikes me that having 99 ways to feel better is a bit lazy – why didn't Jane write 100? But although the book may be one remedy short, it is still worth buying for anyone who is willing to try absolutely anything to cure that morning-after-the-night-before feeling.

Tracy, Brian, *Eat that Frog! 21 Great Ways to Stop Procrastinating and Get More Done in Less Time* (London: Hodder & Stoughton, 2004). To be honest, this book caught my attention because of the title. What does 'Eat that frog' mean? Why would anyone want to eat one in the first place? Anyway, this book has some useful suggestions for managing your time effectively. On Amazon it is loved, receiving endless four- and five-star reviews (but then David Hasselhoff albums regularly receive five stars, so perhaps it's not the most reliable of ratings systems).

Seen a book that should be included in this list? Email me the details at jon.barbuti@ntlworld.com to have it included in the next edition.

DATE DUE
